Continuity and Innovation in Honors College Curricula

Honors Education in Transition

Series Editors: Robert Glover and Katherine O'Flaherty

The landscape of American higher education has changed in notable ways in recent decades. One essential and defining feature of contemporary higher education is the growth of honors education. Honors education offers a means to student self-development, allowing high-performing students a distinctive venue in which they can pursue self-cultivation through expanded educational opportunities. This edited series engages a series of important and timely questions related to the contemporary state of honors education and what promises and challenges exist in its future development.

The first volume in the series engages with the growth in honors education generally, examining the culture around honors education and the challenges and opportunities created by its rapid growth. The second volume in the series turns to curriculum, exploring the various ways that honors educators pursue curricular innovations while navigating the tension between reverence for the past and pedagogical dynamism. The final volume considers how honors education can face larger structural dynamics in higher education—the push for online education, calls to demonstrate "return on investment," and market-based pressures to focus attention on specific fields and skills. Throughout, the series draws upon the insights of seasoned veterans of honors education and new voices to actively consider the future of this important and rapidly growing educational movement.

Titles in the Series

Present Successes and Future Challenges in Honors Education
Continuity and Innovation in Honors College Curricula
Structural Challenges and the Future of Honors Education

Continuity and Innovation in Honors College Curricula

Edited by
Robert W. Glover and
Katherine M. O'Flaherty

ROWMAN & LITTLEFIELD
Lanham • Boulder • New York • London

Published by Rowman & Littlefield
A wholly owned subsidiary of The Rowman & Littlefield Publishing Group, Inc.
4501 Forbes Boulevard, Suite 200, Lanham, Maryland 20706
www.rowman.com

Unit A, Whitacre Mews, 26-34 Stannary Street, London SE11 4AB

Copyright © 2016 by Robert W. Glover and Katherine M. O'Flaherty

All rights reserved. No part of this book may be reproduced in any form or by any electronic or mechanical means, including information storage and retrieval systems, without written permission from the publisher, except by a reviewer who may quote passages in a review.

British Library Cataloguing in Publication Information Available

Library of Congress Cataloging-in-Publication Data Available

ISBN 978-1-4758-2992-1 (cloth : alk. paper)
ISBN 978-1-4758-2993-8 (pbk. alk. paper)
ISBN 978-1-4758-2994-5 (electronic)

∞™ The paper used in this publication meets the minimum requirements of American National Standard for Information Sciences—Permanence of Paper for Printed Library Materials, ANSI/NISO Z39.48-1992.

Printed in the United States of America

Contents

Foreword   vii
James C. McKusick

Acknowledgments   ix

1. Introduction: Curriculum at a Crossroads   1
   Robert W. Glover and Katherine M. O'Flaherty

2. Innovative Methods in Community Engagement for Honors   9
   Cecile Houry

3. Praxis Labs: Theory + Action as a Foundation of a Modern Honors Education   29
   Sylvia Torti and Martha Bradley-Evans

4. The "College" as an Emergent Global Form: One Experience at Starting a Transnational College-to-College Relationship   51
   Catelijne Coopmans, Gregory Clancey, and François G. Amar

5. The Playful Curriculum: Differentiating Honors Education through the Use of Simulation as a Scaffold for Open-ended Course Design   69
   Abby Loebenberg

6. Up the Hill Backward: Meeting the Challenges of Creating a Humanities Lab   89
   Sarah Harlan-Haughey

Index   105

About the Editors and Authors   107

Foreword

Honors education in America today stands at a crossroads. An exceptional period of growth over the last two decades has led to the existence of over one thousand honors programs and colleges in the United States. This burgeoning program growth has led to a substantial investment of new financial resources and an increasing level of personal engagement in honors education by faculty and students at many different kinds of colleges and universities.

Not only the quantity, but also the scale and variety of honors programs have greatly increased in this period. American institutions of higher education have embarked upon a noble experiment to provide the very highest quality of education to suitably talented students through the creation and development of many new honors programs and colleges.

But is this level of growth sustainable? In order to flourish in the resource-constrained and assessment-driven environment of contemporary higher education, many existing honors programs will need to find new and compelling ways to justify their own existence. More than ever before in the history of American higher education, honors faculty members and program directors will need to demonstrate that they offer a distinctive learning environment that is uniquely conducive to improved student learning outcomes and academic success.

Honors education has often presented itself as a conservator of the core values of higher education, particularly through its commitment to a traditional liberal arts curriculum, generally based upon a careful close reading of the "Great Books." At the same time, however, honors programs and colleges throughout the United States have become crucibles of innovation, offering faculty members of all disciplines the freedom to experiment in cutting-edge curricula and new modes of pedagogy that provide honors students with exceptional learning opportunities. At their finest, honors educators have served as the vanguard for new ways of teaching and learning that can fundamentally transform their host institutions.

This book seeks to envision a pathway forward for honors education in these challenging times by fostering the development of authentically innovative honors curriculum. All of the contributors to this book are deeply committed to the progressive and transformative mission of honors education. The volume editors, Robert W. Glover and Katherine M. O'Flaherty, are highly experienced in the design of honors curriculum at their respective institutions, and their introduction to the volume provides a fascinating overview of the challenges and opportunities currently faced by honors educators at a time of sweeping institutional change in higher education. They have assembled a collection of essays that are truly distinctive in scope, originality, and diversity of approach.

Each of the essays in this book offers concrete examples of teaching and learning practices that can potentially transform the very nature of honors education. Many of the contributors propose engaged learning activities that take students beyond the classroom and bring them into contact with the wider world through volunteer service, international education, simulations, "praxis labs," and undergraduate research.

Through various modes of engagement with real-world problems, students in such honors courses learn to take personal responsibility, make ethical decisions, build effective leadership teams, and make a lasting difference to their local and global communities. Taken together, these essays represent a significant contribution to the design of more effective honors courses, offering pathways to better learning outcomes and greater student success in honors programs and colleges throughout the United States.

James C. McKusick
University of Missouri, Kansas City

Acknowledgments

The inception for this edited volume and series was an annual meeting of the National Collegiate Honors Council (NCHC) where the editors discussed the growth of honors in higher education and the opportunities and obstacles that such growth might engender in the future. Initially conceived as a single, edited volume the project grew in scope to an edited series as the editors and publisher realized the diverse array of issues that confront anyone aiming to systematically reckon with the complex landscape of honors in higher education. As the title of the series suggests, our current moment is one of transition—motion from the initial stages of growth to a more systematic accounting of what honors education is, and what educators within this field aspire to see it become in the future.

Since that initial kernel of an idea, many individuals have directly or indirectly helped to prod this edited series from fuzzy concept to tangible set of final products. The editors of this book are extraordinarily grateful to all of the authors in the series who have generously given their time, energy, and expertise. The editors hope that this edited series on teaching and learning in honors will constitute a starting point for a more cohesive, unified, scholarly endeavor. The editors of this book are deeply grateful to them, and hope that future generations of honors educators, scholars, and students will be as well.

The series editors, Robert W. Glover and Katherine M. O'Flaherty, would like to extend their sincere and deep thanks to Tom Koerner, vice president and editorial director, and Bethany Janka, assistant editor, at Rowman & Littlefield. Their editorial vision, commitment to the project, and attention to detail have made this edited series a reality and brought coherence and clarity to the project. Throughout, we have benefited enormously from working with them and have greatly appreciated their enthusiasm and commitment to the project through all of its stages.

On a personal note, Robert W. Glover would like to thank his enormously supportive friends, colleagues, and family (most especially Nicole Brown, Parker Brown, his mother Margaret Glover, and his sisters Carrie and Dianna—all wonderful and important in their own special and unique ways). Katherine M. O'Flaherty would like to thank her colleagues at Barrett, The Honors College at Arizona State University who continually challenge and shape her thinking about higher education. It is a privilege to work with such a brilliant group of people. She'd also like to thank her wonderful friends near and far and her ever supportive parents Patrick and Julia O'Flaherty and sister Patricia O'Flaherty.

Both editors also want to acknowledge and thank their remarkable students who are the inspiration to consider what we are doing and strive to think about ways in which we might do it better. These talented and highly motivated students are what make honors education possible, but beyond this they make this unique domain of teaching incomparably rewarding, valuable, and fulfilling, both professionally and personally.

Chapter 1

Introduction

Curriculum at a Crossroads

Robert W. Glover and Katherine M. O'Flaherty

In 2009, observers began to articulate a series of concerns about Wikipedia, the open-source online encyclopedia that contains an entry for just about everything one could imagine. Though frequently attacked as potentially inaccurate and untrustworthy precisely because of its open authorship, the online resource had grown exponentially. In just eight years it had become the "largest general collection of information ever compiled."[1] Yet as rapidly as it had emerged, Wikipedia seemed mired in stagnation.

Wikipedia's massive army of online volunteer editors was producing new entries at a slower rate and seemed to be equally lethargic in editing or correcting existing entries. Once attracting scores of new "Wikipedians" every day, the resource now seemed to draw fewer volunteers. Novices editing existing entries were frustrated to see their changes revert back, time and time again, to the preexisting content.[2] Wikipedia's radical dynamism and growth seemed to have stalled out. Its heady early days in which thousands of new articles appeared daily now seemed a distant memory.

One journalist trying to make sense of this plateau suggested that it offers far greater lessons than simple insights about the rapidly evolving nature of new internet technologies. Rather, he claimed that Wikipedia is an exemplar of the dangers of growth within organizations more generally. He stated that this is simply what happens when "an idealized community gets too big, it starts becoming dysfunctional. Just like every other human organization."[3]

Nearly any period of initial, rapid growth within an organization or movement eventually sees a more formalized and systematized approach in its subsequent stages. Someone must oversee this process. The tendency to coalesce around elites, who serve as both monitor of the existing regime and "gatekeeper" for new entrants, is a powerful one. As Franz Kafka once bleakly said, "The Revolution evaporates and leaves behind only the slime of a new bureaucracy. The chains of tormented mankind today are made of red tape."[4] Though one need not view such formalization so bleakly, the struggle to maintain dynamism after initial growth is real.

For those embedded in honors education and grappling with its profound growth, perhaps Wikipedia provides an instructive point of comparison for thinking about the future. Honors colleges and programs in the United States have proliferated and honors education itself has evolved in the past two decades—a central point driving much of the analysis and commentary in the first volume in this edited series.[5]

Honors education has become a ubiquitous feature of higher education in the United States. A 2005 report suggested that of the six hundred such programs and college in the United States surveyed at that time, roughly 60 percent had been established since 1994.[6] In the years since 2005, Patricia Smith and Rick Scott found, in the first volume of this series, that the total number of Honors Programs and Colleges has now swelled to over one thousand.[7] At a time when institutions of higher education seem perennially subject to dwindling resources and are told to do "more with less," such growth in the number of honors colleges and programs is truly remarkable.

Yet beyond simply expanding numbers of honors colleges and programs, there has been a considerable effort to articulate the mission of honors education and map out distinctions between an honors college and a program with greater specificity.[8] This has occurred largely through the major professional organization for honors education, the National Collegiate Honors Council (NCHC), and its diversifying and growing membership. Controversial debates about implementation of more formalized assessment models and whether the NCHC should serve as an accreditation body for postsecondary honors education are ongoing.[9]

The first volume in this series offered a collection of provocative and timely essays reflecting upon this wave of growth within honors and its implications for the future of honors education. These essays focused on a series of questions about the priorities of honors education, writ large, given its recent expansion, deepening, and initial steps toward systematization and standardization. Appropriately, given the Wikipedia example at the outset, many of the contributors asked whether those within honors risked becoming victims of their own success. This book, drills down to consider a specific dimension of honors education—its curriculum.

HONORS EDUCATION AND CURRICULUM

Honors education is somewhat unique in that its curriculum can be seen as both a source for innovative change *and* reverence for past tradition—frequently, this happens simultaneously. On the one hand, honors colleges and programs are seen as a venue for pedagogical and curricular innovation. The NCHC envisions mature honors programs as "a laboratory within which faculty feel welcome to experiment with new subjects, approaches, and pedagogies. When proven successful, such efforts in curriculum and pedagogical development can serve as prototypes for initiatives that can become institutionalized across the campus."[10]

Yet this spirit of daring is often set against (or within) the more conservative tradition of a "Great Books" curriculum, singling out a handful of noteworthy foundational texts that form some larger canon of a humanistic, liberal arts education. Grounding in such texts can "nurture a valuable comprehension of human history and humanity's developing sense of the ends of human life and society. It can nurture strong analytic skills and the ability to express oneself clearly and gracefully."[11] This perspective embodies reverence for past great ideas. They serve as the platform students by which arrive at new ideas and put them into practice.

Where innovation and reverence for the past exist side-by-side, great texts are brought into contact with the present in some meaningful way. Such texts may be interrogated for their silences with regard to some historical injustice or inequality. These foundational elements of the "canon" may be the source material by which we examine larger trends over human history—mapping the path that led from an initial assertion to some larger development in our shared past. Or perhaps past writings are read anew with an eye toward the ways in which they speak to contemporary challenges or questions.

The curricular balance between "honors as innovative laboratory" and honors as "historical survey of great ideas" is by no means fixed. Variation in approach depends on the culture of individual programs and colleges, and may also diverge within them as a result of the proclivities of individual instructors. Though honors education may have its roots in classically based, humanistic surveys of "Great Books," its contemporary manifestation is remarkably diverse.[12]

Standardizing the curriculum across honors education, in terms of the subject matter and material engaged, seems somewhat antithetical its larger mission. As Ted Humphrey notes, the prevailing method of seeking continuity in honors education has been to focus on its shared "habits of mind," specifically the "development of specific intellectual dispositions, most importantly, the abilities to read, think, and discuss core issues of human experience analytically and disinterestedly."[13]

In this vein, honors education is less about a common content in terms of subject matter and texts, and more centered on a shared orientation toward what learning and the educational process ought to be. Presumably, one could cultivate the same "habits of mind" articulated above across a variety of different contexts: in the laboratory conducting cutting-edge scientific research, sitting in a circle discussing centuries-old literary or philosophical texts, exploring a city or public space utilizing the "Place-as-Text" pedagogy. This loose mandate can provide educators with atypical freedom and make teaching in honors profoundly rewarding.

HONORS EDUCATION'S "WIKIPEDIA MOMENT?"

One of the greatest questions that faces honors education in the decades to come is whether this loose, decentralized overarching structure will endure. Several broader trends in higher education suggest that this may be a fairly significant challenge. In addition, these developments will impact the question of whether the relative curricular flexibility that programs, colleges, and faculty enjoy will remain.

First, there are dynamics related to the life cycles of the colleges and programs themselves. As noted at the outset, for many institutions, the past few decades have been a time of institutional *formation*—crafting programs, requirements, and curricula at their point of origin. In higher education, as in any institutional setting, dynamism and innovation are easier at the moment of inception than after years of decades have established precedents and helped to craft a culture of norms and expectations. Relatively superficial change and modification may remain possible, but preserving space for dynamism can become incrementally more difficult.

The second challenge relates to scrutiny from above. Remarkably, many if not most of these honors colleges and programs emerged during periods of declining state support and financial stress within higher education more broadly, trends that became critical in the late 2000s.[14] This is no accident; from the point of view of many upper administrators, honors colleges are above all an investment. As Bob Pepperman Taylor notes, "Among the more common goals, at least from the perspective of higher administration, is to make the university more competitive in attracting and retaining high-performing students."[15]

Any investment is going to be scrutinized by those making it, and that scrutiny is likely to become more intense after such an entity has had time to demonstrate results. This is particularly true as honors colleges and programs shift from "bold new experiment" to "established presence on campus." If desired goals in recruitment and retention of students are not being met, those who oversee higher education institutions will likely turn their attention to why this is the case. Pressure may fall upon deans and directors to attend to aspects of the curriculum that appear to be inhibiting success in meeting these goals.

The third way in which honors education's relatively loose curricular structure might encounter resistance relates to assessment. As early as 2008, Lanier wrote, "for better or worse, assessment practices, now inextricably linked to the legitimate call for accountability in higher education have become a significant piece of our academic landscape, and resisting the call to develop best assessment practices for honors education seems a bit like standing on the seashore and repudiating the tide for coming in as it laps around our feet."[16]

What impact widespread calls for accountability and assessment of learning outcomes will have on honors curricula depends largely on the metrics adopted and utilized—one of the key reasons why conversations about assessment can quickly turn contentious. If focused on the "habits of mind" referenced by Humphrey above, the impact on what happens within the classroom could be relatively negligible. If focused toward more rigorous assessment of content acquisition and comprehension, the curricula could change dramatically.

A related matter concerns the curricular standardization that could accompany an effort at accreditation, credentialing, or certification of honors programs and colleges. This is in many ways a reaction to the explosion of honors education in recent years and the enormous diversity encapsulated among institutions that operate under this header. Some within the honors education community have suggested that a way to ensure consistency from one institution to the next is to institute a formal and consequential certification process, overseen by the NCHC.[17]

At present, the formal certification issue remains unresolved. Yet a robust and contentious conversation among members of the larger honors community has begun about its desirability and the impact it would have on individual institutions. Very real fears exist that, though such calls for certification emerge from a place of genuine concern about ensuring quality across institutions, the chilling effect it could have on diversity and innovation in honors education would be real and immediate.

In April 2013, a group of eighteen former presidents of the NCHC reacted to this proposal with a letter of opposition stating, "The bent of those who would pursue the route toward certification or accreditation is to have NCHC validate our honors programs and honors colleges according to some standard. But no such standard exists, and the argument has been cogently made in several NCHC publications that such standardization will stifle creativity, purportedly one of the hallmarks of honors."[18] Formalization of expectations in this way would be a push toward standardization; the impacts for individual curricula remain a serious concern.

The net insight here is that honors colleges and programs are likely to experience increased scrutiny from a variety of directions, internal and external, horizontal and vertical, in the near future. Increasingly, those in honors will need to "justify their own existence." The initial growth period has been one of innovation and diversity. Yet it would be problematic to assume that it will persist indefinitely into the future. The future of curriculum in honors education may be constrained and shaped by forces within and outside institutions that past periods of growth have not.

RETAINING SPACE FOR INNOVATION IN HONORS

In light of the challenging picture of a potentially shrinking space for curricular innovation laid out above, the chapters in this book are striking. Each contribution suggests the ways that honors colleges and programs remain expansive spaces for curricular experimentation and nimble, creative, student-centered pedagogies for which honors education is renowned. These educators and scholars pursue enrichment across a diverse range of high-impact curricular activities—service-learning, study abroad and international education, applied community-based research, and more.

Cecile Houry's contribution articulates the ways that placing service-learning at the center of the honors college curriculum can yield a variety of important benefits. These accrue not only to students who grow academically and personally as they provide tangible benefits to the community. The residents of this community benefit in tangible ways by gaining access to services and resources that they would otherwise lack, but also gaining a sense of connection and reciprocity with the host institution. Furthermore, such partnerships buck historical trends whereby the university constitutes an enclave of privilege in the community in which it resides.

Sylvia Torti and Martha Bradley operate in similar terrain with their applied, problem-based approach to education, entitled "Praxis Labs." Students in these settings work collaboratively to address a pressing social issue for an entire academic year. Half of the year is devoted to understanding the issue in an abstract and conceptual sense, while the second half of the year sees the students work with faculty, community partners and one another to design and implement a solution to the issue.

While the forms of collaboration and engagement in these initial chapters are locally based, we also see internationalization of the curriculum within honors education. This trend is represented here by Catelijne Coopmans and Gregory Clancey from Tembusu College in Singapore and François Amar from the University of Maine Honors College in the United States. The authors discuss the challenges and opportunities associated with building an institutional partnership, and faculty and student exchange program, which literally spans the entire globe.

Abby Loebenberg's chapter focuses on the productive role for "play" in honors education. While play is an essential part of the early childhood curriculum, it is exceedingly rare in secondary and tertiary education. This is despite research in the cognitive sciences that shows that play remains essential to creativity and can aid in knowledge acquisition throughout our lives. Loebenberg considers the possibilities of successfully harnessing the potential of play in honors pedagogy—specifically focusing on simulation and games.

Sarah Harlan-Haughey examines an essential aspect of honors education, mentoring undergraduate research. She documents her attempts to appropriate the lab-based model from the sciences for the purposes of humanities research. Specifically, Harlan-Haughey discusses her collaborative effort to document local "hermits" with a research team of undergraduate students. Her discussion confronts the challenges of mentoring undergraduate students in conducting humanities research and her agile attempts to navigate these challenges while meeting professional and institutional expectations and ensuring an enriching opportunity for students.

These chapters all suggest that honors education remains a space for curricular innovation and can serve as a laboratory for challenging, unconventional, and fundamentally novel modes of teaching and learning. Throughout, the educators featured here ground their discussion in personal experience, the broader context of honors and disciplinary research, and the larger trends in the development of honors education discussed in this introductory chapter. The result is an impressive statement of what honors curricula can be, and the motivations that drive those within honors to embrace novel teaching frameworks and content.

KEY IDEAS IN THIS CHAPTER

- Curricula in honors education has tended to be focused on shared "habits of mind" rather than any consistent content or subject matter—a freedom that has inspired innovation.
- The growth witnessed in honors education sets in motion a series of forces, and an enhanced degree of scrutiny, that could foster a more formalized and standardized curricular structure.
- The chapters presented in this edited series demonstrate the ways that continued innovation and dynamism are possible, despite larger trends toward formalization.

NOTES

1. Farhad Manjoo, "Is Wikipedia a Victim of Its Own Success?" *TIME*, accessed January 5, 2016, http://content.time.com/time/magazine/article/0,9171,1924492,00.html.

2. Talk of the Nation. 2016. "Wikipedia: A 'Victim of Its Own Success?'" *NPR.org*, accessed February 5. http://www.npr.org/templates/story/story.php?storyId=113128568.

3. Ibid.

4. Gustav Janouch, *Conversations with Kafka*, 2nd Ed. (New York: New Directions, 1971), p. 121.

5. Robert W. Glover and Katherine O'Flaherty, Eds., *Honors Education in Transition: Present Successes and Future Challenges in Honors Education* (New York: Rowman and Littlefield, 2016).

6. Joan Digby, *Peterson's Honor Programs and Colleges: The Official Guide of the National Collegiate Honors Council* (Lawrenceville, NJ: Thomson Peterson, 2005), p. 5.

7. Patricia Smith and Rick Scott, "Growth and Evolution of Collegiate Honors Education in the United States," Ed. Robert W. Glover and Katherine O'Flaherty, *Honors Education in Transition: Present Successes and Future Challenges in Honors Education* (New York: Rowman and Littlefield, 2016), Ch. 2.

8. National Collegiate Honors Council, "Basic Characteristics of a Fully Developed Honors Program," accessed June 19, 2014, http://nchchonors.org/faculty-directors/basic-characteristics-of-a-fully-developed-honors-program; National Collegiate Honors Council, "Definition of Honors Education," accessed May 13, 2015, http://nchchonors.org/wp-content/uploads/2014/02/Definition-of-Honors-Education.pdf.

9. Cheryl Achterberg, "Honors Assessment and Evaluation," *Journal of the National Collegiate Honors Council* 7, no. 1 (2006): 37–40; Ann Marie Guzy, "*Harry Potter* and the Specter of Honors Accreditation," *Journal of the National Collegiate Honors Council* 12, no. 2 (2011): 85–90.

10. National Collegiate Honors Council, "Basic Characteristics of a Fully Developed Honors Program."

11. Ted Humphrey, "The Genesis of an Idea," in *The Honors College Phenomenon*, Ed. Peter C. Sederberg (Lincoln, NE: National Collegiate Honors Council, 2008), p. 16.

12. See Smith and Scott, "Growth and Evolution of Collegiate Honors Education in the United States," for an overview of the historical emergence of contemporary honors education.

13. Humphrey, "The Genesis of an Idea," p. 17.

14. Jeffrey J. Selingo, "Colleges Struggling to Stay Afloat," *New York Times*, April 12, 2013, accessed February 7, 2016 from http://www.nytimes.com/2013/04/14/education/edlife/many-colleges-and-universities-face-financial-problems.html.

15. Bob Pepperman Taylor, "How to Create an Honors College," in *The Honors College Phenomenon*, Ed. Peter C. Sederberg (Lincoln, NE: National Collegiate Honors Council, 2008), p. 97.

16. Gregory W. Lanier, "Towards Reliable Honors Assessment," *Journal of the National Collegiate Honors Council* (Spring/Summer) 9, no. 1 (2008): 82.

17. National Collegiate Honors Council, "Preliminary Certification Proposal," accessed February 7, 2016, http://nchchonors.org/news/preliminary-certification-proposal/.

18. Ibid.

Chapter 2

Innovative Methods in Community Engagement for Honors

Cecile Houry

Historically, institutions of higher education have failed to develop healthy and productive relationships with their surrounding communities. Instead of embracing these communities, most universities have, until recently, focused inward, emphasizing research, publication, material resources, and prestige. This approach is often described as the "Ivory Tower" or the "town and gown" phenomenon.[1]

A combination of socioeconomic, political, and educational changes has progressively shattered this model and today, a growing number of institutions of higher learning recognize the essentiality of community engagement for students' personal and academic growth and success and for collaboratively developing healthy neighborhoods.

Honors programs/colleges, specifically designed to offer curricula of challenging seminars with cutting-edge pedagogy fostering intellectual curiosity, critical thinking, interdisciplinary cooperation, and leadership training, are strategically positioned to take the lead on these emerging community engagement objectives.

After a brief historical overview, this chapter focuses on the community partnership that the Honors College at Florida International University (FIU) has forged with its neighboring city of Sweetwater to examine theoretical points, potential programs, and resulting opportunities/challenges of using a geographical locus as a classroom. By doing so, this chapter offers an experiential learning engagement model that can be embraced or duplicated and reflects what honors colleges/programs of the future should look like.

HISTORICAL BACKGROUND

With rising educational costs, diminishing federal and state financial support, changing student populations and expectations, constantly evolving technologies, and shrinking job opportunities, higher education is in crisis. Private and public institutions alike are at a crossroads, forced to reexamine their mission, redefine success, and develop new success metrics while spending an increasing amount of time, money, and energy raising funds.

Arising in the midst of this necessary reinvention is what should have always been at the center of all discussions but was forgotten for most of the twentieth century—the role of education in preparing tomorrow's citizens and leaders, in maintaining democratic ideals, and in solving pressing local, national, and global societal problems. A brief overview of key historical episodes sheds light on the development of the American university and the role political leaders, educators, and social reformers intended higher educational institutions to play in society.

The establishment of land-grant colleges and universities and the passage of the Morrill Acts of 1862 and 1890 reflect the postbellum belief that educational institutions should serve the community. The goal of these two acts, for instance, was to ensure land-grant institutions provided training in agriculture, military tactics, and mechanical arts, thus offering the working classes access to education and practical knowledge that had direct relevance to their daily lives and to the growing industrial society.

The Progressive Era, a period marked by strong social activism and political reform, played an essential role in the concept of urban community development. Educational theories linked the role of education and the formation and maintenance of democratic societies. One of the leading theorists, John Dewey, argued that the traditional private educational system was outdated, restricted to the elite social class, and focused too exclusively on a pedagogical curriculum based on cultural heritage, classical studies, established standards, and strict rules of conduct.

In this system, the educators' responsibility was to transmit information and rules onto the next generation and students were passive receptors, deprived of critical reflection, experiential learning, and real life application opportunities.[2] This is why Dewey created the Laboratory School, later renamed the "Dewey School."

Dewey considered this space a community of active learners and a laboratory for educational thinking and experiments, linking education, experience, character, engagement, and democratic ideals. This was for him the only way to ensure students would learn and grow and communities would remain civil, democratic societies.

Jane Addams's work also embodies the era's attempts to bridge academic and community divides. In 1889, after visiting a London settlement house,

Addams and Ellen Gates Starr founded Hull House in Chicago's West Side. They relied on educated women, generally restricted to the "domestic sphere" to volunteer and provide social and educational opportunities for neighboring working-class men and women, mostly recent Eastern Europe immigrants.

Hull House offered a wide range of opportunities including classes focused on a traditional knowledge-based curriculum, classes teaching practical skills and knowledge, social and cultural events, children's activities, and athletic programs. Addams and Starr also used Hull House to research societal issues and disseminate the results to relevant authorities so policies could be changed accordingly. Hull House's holistic approach to societal issues came to be described as Addams' "three R's"—residence, research, and reform. The "three R's" clearly linked people, scholarly research, public policy, and the creation of more democratic societies.

This approach to education, community, and democracy was not implemented broadly over the years and for most of the twentieth century, institutions of higher education failed to develop healthy and productive relationships with their surrounding communities, choosing to focus on research, publication, and academic prestige. Recently, however, growing numbers of institutions have reinserted community engagement into their missions and strategic plans.[3] To understand the impact on honors programs/colleges, it is essential to consider what community engagement in higher education means today and why it is again driving pedagogical priorities.

In 2005, the Carnegie Foundation, which focuses on advancing teaching and learning, launched a classification to recognize institutional commitment to deepening the practice of service and strengthening bonds between campus and community via teaching, researching, and serving.[4] The classification application lays outs the definition, indicators, metrics, and success of engagement:

> Community engagement describes collaboration between institutions of higher education and their larger communities (local, regional/state, national, global) for the mutually beneficial exchange of knowledge and resources in a context of partnership and reciprocity. The purpose of community engagement is the partnership of college and university knowledge and resources with those of the public and private sectors to enrich scholarship, research, and creative activity; enhance curriculum, teaching and learning; prepare educated, engaged citizens; strengthen democratic values and civic responsibility; address critical societal issues; and contribute to the public good.[5]

This definition encapsulates what progressive reformers pushed forward late in the nineteenth century. For Dr. Ira Harkavy, founding director of the Barbara and Edward Netter Center for Community Partnerships at the University of Pennsylvania and national expert on community engagement, this is what today's universities, especially urban ones, should focus on for four main reasons.[6]

First comes self-interest—it is easier, cheaper, and faster for an institution to maintain campus safety, cleanliness, and attractiveness when the surrounding neighborhoods are well governed and inhabited by educated, empowered, and productive residents. Second, a lack of engagement costs universities in terms of positive public relations, political relationships, and community support. Third, being engaged allows the institution to fulfill its mission to teach, advance the corpus of knowledge, and become solution center for surrounding communities.

Lastly, and most broadly of all, engagement promotes civic consciousness, which is positive for students, institutions, and communities: "The beneficiaries of investing in such learning are not just students or higher education itself; the more civic-oriented that colleges and universities become, the greater their overall capacity to spur local and global economic vitality, social and political well-being, and collective action to address public problems."[7]

The Carnegie Foundation conducted four application cycles (2006, 2008, 2010, 2015) and 361 institutions received the engagement classification. The foundation released the following data about the 2015 cycle: 241 first-time applicants requested the application, 133 submitted it, and eighty-three obtained the classification. Also, 188 campuses were eligible for reclassification, 162 submitted an application, and 157 were reclassified. Among the first-time recipients, forty-seven are public institutions, and thirty-six are private.

Of those institutions receiving Carnegie's Basic Classification, twenty-nine are classified as research universities, twenty-eight are master's colleges/universities, seventeen are baccalaureate colleges, three are community colleges, and five have a specialized focus—arts, medicine, and other health professions. They represent thirty-three states and U.S. territories.[8] This data shows that a significant number of universities have progressively embraced Ira Harkavy's vision and that community engagement is now a widespread phenomenon.

THE BENEFITS OF A GEOGRAPHICAL ENGAGEMENT MODEL FOR HONORS

Since 2009, Florida International University (FIU), located in Miami, has encouraged community engagement at an unprecedented level. This public, urban, minority-serving university, boasting 54,000 students and over six thousand faculty and staff, created an Office of Engagement, appointed a Vice President and several program coordinators, budgeted funds for that office, and launched multiple initiatives and partnerships.

FIU's engagement priorities are reflected in its 2010 strategic plan, which includes "educating undergraduate students who understand and commit to their civic responsibilities;" "building a distinguished faculty and staff who collaborate with each other and with community leaders to explore creative solutions to local, regional, national, and global problems;" and "building collaborative university/community relationships that employ the intellectual capital of the university to solve community problems and . . . enhance the intellectual development of the community through life-long learning opportunities."[9] FIU obtained the Carnegie Foundation Engagement Classification in 2010.

The FIU Honors College, a center of excellence preparing some of the university's best and brightest to become well-rounded individuals and leaders in their fields and communities, was among the first FIU academic units to boldly embrace and institutionalize community engagement via a geographical community partnership. In 2009, the College approached the mayor of the City of Sweetwater and "adopted" this underserved city of roughly 15,000 mostly Hispanic residents located directly across from the university's main entrance.[10, 11]

This innovative partnership exemplified Dewey's and Harkavy's educational recommendations, since it was designed to engage students in projects that improve the quality of life of local residents while providing students and faculty with advanced academic and research opportunities. Such experiences help students to develop leadership skills and practice civic engagement and provide, through internships, opportunities for students to learn about the management and governance of a small city.

In an even broader sense, these steps are the beginning of an effort to integrate the university and its members more fully into the local community. It is important to note that before this partnership, the relationship between the university and Sweetwater had historically been adversarial and distrustful.

After six years, students, faculty, university, and community participation, collaboration, and feedback made it evident that such a geographical approach is beneficial and one which other honors institutions could undertake. Such efforts offer honors programs/colleges opportunities to fulfill their educational mission, provide an honors experience for students, build an honors culture, align with their institution's mission and strategic goals, all while serving as an efficient and powerful marketing tool.

Honors Colleges and Programs' Educational Mission

The renewed higher education institutional emphasis on community engagement is positive for honors programs/colleges and should be embraced because the teaching, researching, and service opportunities that come with community engagement fit perfectly the definition of honors education that the National Collegiate Honors Council (NCHC) uses:

> Honors education is characterized by in-class and extracurricular activities that are measurably broader, deeper, or more complex than comparable learning experiences typically found at institutions of higher education. Honors experiences include a distinctive learner-directed environment and philosophy, provide opportunities that are appropriately tailored to fit the institution's culture and mission, and frequently occur within a close community of students and faculty.[12]

The NCHC also specifies that traditional honors education includes some of the following modes of learning: research and creative scholarship, breadth and enduring questions ("multi- or interdisciplinary learning"), service-learning and leadership, experiential learning, and/or learning communities.[13] Associating a program/college with a community, defined by a geographical perimeter (as opposed to a center, organization, or cause) provides room for all these learning modes. In collaboration with the City and community partners, the FIU Honors College has launched, inter alia, several kinds of programs and initiatives.

Extracurricular Activities

Students can volunteer for onetime city events (Thanksgiving Bash, a Spanish Month Reception, clean up days, philanthropic endeavors, etc.) or ongoing programs (tutoring sessions, citizenship classes, computer classes for seniors, athletic programs, and lunches with seniors). For the latter, students volunteer on the same day and time every week throughout a semester.

Students can apply for internships. Every semester, eight to ten positions focusing on government administration, grant and economic development, and media and public relations are available at the Mayor's Office and other governmental sites. These twenty hour-per-week internships are unpaid but highly educational and greatly increase the chances of students and recent grads finding employment.[14] At least three interns have then been employed full-time by the City.

Students can also come up with their own ideas for programs or community solutions and implement them. For example, one student group set up a campus Halloween drive, collecting costumes and then distributing them to lower income Sweetwater residents.

Finally, the Honors College works to involve the community in university programs and events, such as a sponsoring a joint football game tailgate, having the elementary school choir sing the National Anthem at Honors College events, or inviting residents to lectures and programs.

Curricular Initiatives

The NCHC specifies that most honors courses will aim at helping students develop effective written and oral communication skills and an ability to analyze and synthesize a broad range of material; understand how scholars think about problems, formulate hypotheses, research those problems and draw conclusions; help students understand how creative artists approach the creative process and produce an original work; become more independent and critical thinkers, demonstrate abilities to use knowledge and logic when discussing an issue or an idea, and consider consequences of their ideas, for themselves, for others, and for society.[15]

The FIU Honors College uses three approaches regarding course offerings, all aligned with the objectives listed above. First, the FIU Honors College utilizes service-learning, which Campus Compact, a national coalition of colleges and universities committed to campus-based civic engagement, defines as a pedagogy that "incorporates community work into the curriculum, giving students real-world learning experiences that enhance their academic learning while providing a tangible benefit for the community."[16] The Honors College, via public speaking, website, social media, and publications, showcases its engagement courses and emphasizes their benefits, thus encouraging other faculty to develop service-learning courses and offering Sweetwater as a project site.

A required freshman class, for example, focuses on leadership theories and skills and puts them into practice through "An Evening with the Arts," a community event held at the local elementary school. Students form working committees, collaborate with the Sweetwater Elementary art and music teachers, raise funds, secure sponsors, and manage the event, which includes an art exhibition, musical performances, brief speeches by FIU and Sweetwater officials, and a dinner for the three hundred or so Sweetwater residents and FIU members in attendance. At the end of the semester, students reflect on this experience as it applies to leadership.

Second, the FIU Honors College utilizes service-research, its term for initiatives involving students in data collection, practical reasoning, and problem-solving strategies to help address current community issues. The concept takes students a step beyond service-learning, requiring intensive research on an identified issue, proposing a feasible solution, and in most cases, implementing that solution. Community-based research principles serve as a foundation, but are adapted for a multidisciplinary undergraduate population in a class setting.[17]

In 2011, the Honors College launched a course using this approach to address some of the social, cultural, economic, political, environmental, educational, and health problems in Sweetwater. Students conduct research about community partnerships and about the city. They identify issues and, based on their majors and interests, select one. They then work as a team with the instructor to identify university faculty members or administrators, city officials, nonprofit leaders, or corporate agents who can help them develop creative solutions, initiate their implementation, assess their impact and reflect on the experience.

Third, the FIU Honors College also utilizes independent research. The Honors College offers a one-year research seminar, resulting in a thesis and conference presentation, for which students meet every other week, are paired with a faculty mentor, and develop a project. Students interested in community affairs can focus their research on the City of Sweetwater.

Such programs, activities, and courses allow honors programs/colleges to fulfill their educational mission and to create transformational honors experiences for its students, in the form of reflective and introspective moments that allow students to increase their self-awareness and awareness of others.

Honors Experience for Students

Anthropologist Clifford Geertz argued, after witnessing several cockfights during a trip to a Balinese village in 1958, that "cultural forms [such as a cockfight] can be treated as texts, as imaginative works built out of social materials."[18] For Geertz, the cockfight represents "a simulation of the social matrix."[19] A cockfight is not just a cockfight, but a view of Balinese society in action. The cockfight illuminates the different Balinese social classes, the role of the government, the way people relate to each other and to the government, what matters to these people, and so on.

In 1963, sport historian C. L. R. James argued the same in his acclaimed work, *Beyond a Boundary*.[20] This book is about cricket. But because James places this game within the context of society as a whole, it is about much more. It is about the West Indies, colonialism, poverty, social classes, loyalty, power, and control. In other words, "cricket is James's microscope and through it he magnifies whole areas of life and thought. He presents cricket as both sport and metaphor, the property of colonizers and colonized, in which struggles over culture, power, hegemony, and resistance are played out."[21]

Cities function along the same lines. Similar to Geertz's Balinese cockfight and James's cricket game, they offer a "simulation of the social matrix." As such, they are contested spaces and such spaces are not neutral. Through political, economic, social, and cultural maneuvers, spaces are assigned certain characteristics and values that can include class, racial, or gender statuses. The dominant social class is often able to impose its values and expectations on members of other classes, making these values and expectations the socially desirable standards.

A body, like a space, is not neutral; it is a sociocultural product constructed through power relations. In other words, a body is not only a representation of sex, but also of ideologies. Institutions, such as schools, religious establishments, the state, the military, our working places, and even our families, normalize these ideologies. Because bodies and spaces are cultural products, they are never static and a range of power relations are constantly being played out, altering the existing race, gender, and class roles and definitions. Entering that space and observing public behaviors is therefore essential to understand how human relationships and societies are formed and maintained.

A geographical community partnership, then, allows honors programs/colleges to use the selected city as a laboratory for all the activities, programs, and courses mentioned previously, but also as a text to be observed, experienced, questioned, and reflected upon—all key elements of honors education. The City as Text© methodology developed in 1976 by Bernice Braid, director of the honors program at Long Island University, is an excellent model for this, and one promoted by the NCHC since then. Braid's belief is that "a crucial asset of active learning is providing a mechanism for disrupting our habits and assumptions."[22] City or Place as Text is an efficient way to do that.

Students, in small teams, are sent to a place (city, campus, park, etc.) for a specific amount of time. They are given a few instructions, such as using public transportation, buying lunch, asking directions, etc. Braid mentions that during this phase, students "engage in focused observations: Who plays what games at school? On the street? In parks? What are the private uses of public spaces in train stations, parks, in front of museums, in subways? How do others respond to these uses? How do you, as observer, respond? How do you feel while watching others? Why do you have these feelings?"[23] The second part of the assignment is to reflect and write about this experience.

This experiential learning activity allows students to observe and map public behaviors, but also to become aware of the influence of "the angle of vision, angle of inquiry, kinds of questions, and context created by one's own presence in the scene."[24] By so doing, students learn about themselves—the lens through which they observe and the perspective they bring to the picture.

Looking at the reflective pieces written by City or Place-as-Text students, Braid concluded that learning outcomes fell into three categories: "First, expanding the intellectual side of their life; second, understanding the power of community; and Third, developing a concept of self, both in relation to the community they are in and as unique individuals."[25]

In *Introduction to Community Development*, Robinson and Green's reasoning goes a step farther, linking experiential learning to the development of self and global citizenship:

> Learning grounded in local context and experience has the best chance of engaging students intellectually, academically, and civically. Place-based education is [. . .] an acknowledgement of the interdependence among all people in all places. Acquiring the skills to analyze and understand local issues affecting communities leads to an enhanced capacity to understand similar issues at a global level. Therefore, although local in its orientation, place-based education is simultaneously global in its scope.[26]

Experiential, integrative, and transformational learning methods, then, are crucial to educate and develop well-rounded young leaders in the twenty-first century, providing them with opportunities inside and outside of the classroom to experience concrete examples of social phenomena, gain "real-world" knowledge and insights, learn how to apply practical reasoning to solve community problems, develop new skills and knowledge, gain leadership ability, enhance moral character development, and inculcate civic responsibilities. These learning outcomes allow honors institutions to fulfill their missions but also develop a strong and unique honors culture.

Build an Honors Culture

In "The Culture of Honors," George Mariz looks at how the word "culture" has historically been defined. He then puts forward three kinds of cultural or social bonds and organization. First, common-interest cultures—people join, with a low entry price, based on allegiance to a team, a social organization, a cause, or so on. Second, identity cultures—admission usually comes by virtue of birth, ethnicity, residence, occupation, or a similar circumstance. And third, voluntary cultures—membership is neither automatic nor open to everyone. Price and requirements for entry are high and rewards correspondingly great.[27]

For Mariz, honors programs/colleges are built on elements of these categories. Defining a culture as "a group of people who pursue a common aim, and for honors this means specifically students and faculty who pursue an academic aim," he explains that it is a voluntary culture in the sense that it is exclusive, and in some cases, perceived as elitist.[28]

Specific requirements are necessary for students to remain members. Membership often mandates more courses, work, and/or volunteer hours. There are unique rewards, like priority registration or an "honors" designation on the diploma. The academic relationship with faculty members may be closer.

The program/college may offer opportunities only for its members. Honors programs/colleges also represents an identity culture in the sense that students choose to associate with those having a similar interest in intense learning. Finally, it is also a culture of common interest. Mariz defines the intellectual common interest as follows:

> The culture of honors above all encourages, indeed demands, fearless questioning, and just as there is no field that escapes its purview, there is likewise no question it fears to ask. It is, above all, a culture of intellectual effort. Everyone who enters it must do so with a commitment to hard work, a spirit of inquiry, and a willingness to ask the hard question, often the uncomfortable question, and to live with the consequences of receiving an unintended or unpleasant answer.[29]

In "Creating an Honors Culture," Jim Ford touches on a similar component of the honors culture, arguing that the common quest for intellectual knowledge and discussions unites honors students:

> Perhaps motivation alone is not the dominant trait of honors students, but a certain kind of motivation—a genuine joy in learning—is as vital to honors culture as intellectual risk-taking. It's not just a willingness to take risks that leads to great interdisciplinary work, say, although that is certainly necessary; honors students *want* to learn about subjects outside their major; they have a *passion* for knowledge and for wisdom. That passion for learning is an indispensable component of honors culture and, like intellectual risk-taking, is characteristic of both honors faculty and honors students.[30]

Community engagement partnerships are excellent vehicles for developing a coherent honors culture because they rally students, faculty, and staff around one project, or set of projects, involving teaching, learning, and serving. Most honors students are naturally involved in community programs and activities. It is not rare to see them lead student governments and organize Relay for Life or Dance Marathon events. Yet these individual acts do not bring them together as honors students. Community partnerships do.

Similar to honors programs/colleges, community partnerships are built on the culture categories Mariz mentioned—one needs to be a member of the honors program/college to participate, there are requirements for participation and resume-building, and a common community-driven interest. Opting for a geographical community partnership therefore brings all the honors constituents together and offers opportunities to share, learn, contribute, and feel part of a very unique group and project—all building a sense of belonging and pride about the self and about the honors program/college.

EFFICIENT MARKETING TOOL

Having students engaged in the community in a way that increases their self-awareness, educates them about civic responsibilities and global citizenship, provides them with leadership opportunities, and impacts the local residents positively is an efficient marketing tool because it supports the institutional mission and strategic goals of most twenty-first-century universities. As stated earlier, FIU's 2010 strategic plan lists several goals related to students, faculty, staff, and institutional engagement with the community. By partnering with a neighboring city, the Honors College has positioned itself in alignment with the university's mission and as a model program for the university to showcase.

Developing a partnership with a specific geographical area is also an efficient public relations and marketing tool because it is measurable. As mentioned previously, honors students are generally more engaged in their education than non-honors students, often at the forefront of the student government, service-oriented clubs, and charity events such as Relay for Life, Dance Marathon, and Heart Walk. Though extremely valuable, these endeavors are individual and not honors-based acts. It is therefore difficult or impossible to quantify the students' engagement level and its impact on an organization or community.

Community engagement in higher education is still not measured efficiently or systematically. Campus Compact's 2011 Executive Summary, which showcases the results of its annual membership survey, highlights this: "Relatively few campuses track activity in a systematic way, and even fewer have mechanisms in place for assessing impact. Only 32 percent of responding campuses track engagement activity campus-wide, while specific campus units track activity at another 55 percent. On 13 percent of campuses, there is no mechanism in place to track engagement efforts at all."[31]

Today's higher educational world is about metrics. What cannot be shown and quantified gets easily omitted from reports to university presidents, boards of trustees and governors, the media, and granting agencies. Campus Compact points this out arguing that "if campuses do not have a firm grasp of what they are accomplishing in the community, they are failing to capitalize on a huge opportunity to highlight not only the value of their own work, but also the role of higher education as an agent of positive change."[32] And that impacts the university in several areas, including recruitment, retention, graduation, funding, and public relations.

Similarly, while honors programs/colleges adopting a geographical approach may not always be able to measure impact, the partnership provides an easy, efficient, and sustainable way to measure engagement levels. The staff member(s) coordinating the different activities and programs can quantify them in terms of hours of service provided, number of students involved, and number of people reached.

When the community work involved in all the courses, programs, and events are added, it provides a good picture of the program's community engagement and the impact on the community in terms of category and quantity of services offered. This is a valuable public and marketing tool, one that makes it easier to reach different audiences.

At the internal level, the Sweetwater Partnership became a flagship program for the Honors College. Articles about it appeared in the university newspaper and the Honors College and FIU magazines. Through short videos and public forums, the president of the university showcased the program as exemplary of FIU's goals. Rapidly, other units—fraternities, colleges, athletic teams, faculty, student organizations—heard about the partnership and reached out to Honors to see how they might contribute, creating mutually beneficial collaborative and interdisciplinary opportunities.

At the external level, such a partnership is essential to reach critical audience groups. First, the local community. The Honors College-Sweetwater partnership has been featured several times in the *Miami Herald*, the major local newspaper. Also, Honors College volunteers wear identifying t-shirts when volunteering in the community, which increases visibility and emphasizes the institution's commitment to community engagement.

Second, such a partnership helps with funding and governmental agencies. The Honors College and the City of Sweetwater have applied for several grants related to this partnership. In 2013, FIU and the City were awarded an $11.4 million TIGER grant from the U.S. Department of Transportation "to support an innovative package of technology, streetscaping and transit improvements to connect the town of Sweetwater with Florida International University (FIU)."[33]

When applying, FIU featured the Honors College's partnership with Sweetwater to showcase the solid and sustainable relationship, trust, and work already in place. What is more, the FIU Honors College is involved in portions of the grant that will involve students even further.

Finally, a partnership is an efficient and powerful academic marketing tool. Many students have showcased their community research and projects via conference posters or panel sessions. Faculty and staff have also presented at conferences and written articles or chapters about their community work, thus indirectly marketing the partnership to regional and national audiences.

The Honors College, then, because of its self-motivated student body, interdisciplinary pedagogical approaches, and emphasis on developing well-rounded citizens and leaders, has been in the right strategic position to take the lead on community collaborations and has demonstrated the value of geographical partnerships. Launching and maintaining this kind of community partnership, however, is not without challenges.

Challenges to a Geographical Approach to Engagement for Honors

A Partnership—Why, Who, What, How

Launching such a partnership is time-consuming. Institutions of higher education are often in a hurry to start a new program and see it make headlines. This does not work well with this kind of partnership, as it requires substantial expenditures of time and energy, especially in the early phases. Before reaching out to any potential partner, for instance, honors programs/colleges must do some introspective and reflective work.

Such institutions must ask themselves "Why a partnership? What goals can be achieved with a partnership for students, faculty, program, university, and the community?" From here, they can consider, whether this is the right time to launch such an initiative. For instance, are there currently the infrastructure and human resources to manage the initiative? Would such a partnership be aligned with the university's strategic plan? Are there other significant initiatives that need to be the focus of publicity, effort, and strategic goals?

At this point, an honors program or college must consider its student population. Who are the students? Are they mostly commuters who are only somewhat aware and emotionally attached to the campus and its vicinity? Are they mostly out-of-state students whose concerns and energy are not locally-oriented? Do they live on campus? How do they view their relationship to various communities and especially to the campus and its neighboring cities? What is their level of civic responsibility and engagement? Are they full-time students? Nontraditional students? Do they have responsibilities such as jobs and families to support?

All of this needs to be taken into account when choosing the kind of partnership one wants. For instance, if the students are primarily full-time students with part-time jobs and family responsibilities, the time they can devote to volunteering, interning, or researching away from campus is going to be limited. A city or organization located in close proximity to campus can therefore be highly appropriate for success.

Lastly, honors programs and colleges must ask what kind of partnership is wanted. Is the institution looking at partnering with a single organization—a school, nonprofit, corporation? Should it rather partner with a few organizations tackling a specific topic or field, such as education, homelessness, immigration, etc.? Or should it partner with a neighborhood or city? Opting to partner with a neighborhood or city can make sense for honors programs/colleges, as demonstrated, especially because it allows for a holistic, interdisciplinary and all-encompassing approach.

Also, in accordance with the four characteristics that Jessica Barnes et al. emphasize, they must "be grounded in meaningful and sustainable research partnerships, focus on community capacity building, . . . involve long-term relationships with communities, and create collaborative networks in the community and university."[34]

Selecting a Partner

Once one has considered all this, one needs to identify which entity in the community would be open to such a partnership. Kerry Strand argues that for a partnership to work, it is necessary that "partners share a worldview, partners agree about goals and strategies, and partners have mutual trust and mutual respect."[35] It is important to note that the partnership the FIU Honors College developed with Sweetwater would probably not be as successful in a well-to-do community.

Developing a Trustful Relationship

Trustful relationships and reciprocity must be established with the adopted community, which takes time. Communities are sometimes reluctant to let educational units in, fearing that their priorities might not necessarily benefit residents. Several universities have, in the past, been heavily criticized for overtaking neighborhoods or cities, changing them in ways that help the institution but make life more difficult for the local population.

One reason the partnership between the FIU Honors College and Sweetwater has worked so well is that the Honors College opted for a bottom-up approach, creating a collective process through which the local community and its key constituents participated in the decision-making, strategic planning, and priority-setting meetings related to the partnership. This goes a long way toward establishing the trust needed for success.

Time Constraints

The time necessary to maintain, assess, and expand the existing partnership is significant. A full-time program coordinator or director is ideal but not always feasible. This limits the programs and improvements the college or program can launch. It also forces the college to be careful about expansion in order not to sacrifice the quality of the services and educational experiences for a more visible and marketable growth. Time is also a challenge because campus and community function on different schedules. It is often difficult to obtain the planning time necessary from community members busy addressing residential and governmental emergencies.

Moreover, when the community voices a specific need and hope that the honors program/college can address it, it is often a last-minute request that does not provide much turn-around time for the program/college to jump through bureaucratic hoops and deliver. Finally, for curricular activities, time is restricted to class and a few hours of homework per week so the level of engagement and possible impact on the community is also restricted. Clear communication about time expectations, availability, need, and restraints is therefore essential.

Human Resources

Human sustainability is an obstacle. The FIU Honors College, for instance, does not offer credit-bearing internship classes and does not require participation in the partnership. Students are only required to perform twenty hours of community service, anywhere, per academic year. The partnership therefore relies on students wanting to get engaged in the community and finding the time to do so. Student participation is not guaranteed or constant; yet without it, the partnership would cease. This means that promoting, recruiting and training students is essential.

Similarly, the partnership has to be functioning well and be attractive enough for faculty members to want to participate, either through personal research and publication on community engagement topics or through the development of classes involving students in service-learning or service-research projects. This is not always an easy sell, since such classes differ significantly from traditional classes.

Richard A. Couto observes that "a learning community can be far messier than a command-and-control classroom."[36] Braid also points to the different work requirements for engagement courses: "The work one does in this kind of education is a different kind of work, involving less preparation of lecture materials and more responsiveness to individual students. In this process, faculty often do more work after class than before, tracking down answers to questions students have raised."[37]

So the faculty must be willing, understanding, and flexible enough to teach this kind of course well. On the community side, the programs, initiatives, and human capital must also be sustainable. Partners have to commit, at a minimum, to being reachable and available, and resident participation has to be obtained for most programs.

Financial Resources

Financial sustainability is one of the most important obstacles. It is difficult—and again, time-consuming—to find reliable and long-term funding sources for community partnerships. The Honors College cannot spend any part of its budget on Sweetwater because its funds are both limited and restricted.[38] Yet most activities or programs do require a modicum of funding every year. The girls' athletic program in place at the Sweetwater Elementary School is costly, for example, because student volunteer need to be fingerprinted through the Miami-Dade Public School Office.[39] Applying for grants is often the most efficient way to sustain such partnerships.

Institutions of higher learning are increasingly encouraging their different schools, centers, and departments to be locally engaged. With experiential and transformative learning and cutting-edge methods, honors programs/colleges are strategically positioned to take the lead on such projects. The Honors College at FIU has successfully done so. Its partnership with the City of Sweetwater provides a valuable model in terms of educational benefits to students, the number and quality of its programs and activities, the groundbreaking relationships it has established, and the successes it has achieved in dealing with inherent challenges.

This model is not unique to FIU's circumstances, and can be duplicated and adapted to other communities. Community partnerships fit the definition of honors education perfectly, provide unique life-changing honors experience, and help develop a strong honors culture. They also place the honors program/college strategically within the university setting and represent an effective public relations and marketing tool locally and nationally. And importantly, they are the ideal example of what honors education is about and should therefore be at the center of any discussions about the future of honors education and what honors colleges and programs should look like going forward.

KEY IDEAS IN THIS CHAPTER

- Community engagement presents an opportunity for colleges and universities to bridge the gap between the university and the community, serving a publicly-oriented mission outlined by educational reformers such as John Dewey and Jane Addams.
- Engagement and service-learning provide educational opportunities for students and faculty, while simultaneously providing tangible benefits for communities and their members.
- Honors Colleges are uniquely poised to take advantage of the potential of these geographically-based partnerships, evident here in the collaboration between Florida International University's Honors College and the community of Sweetwater.

NOTES

1. Lawrence L. Martin, Hayden Smith, and Wende Phillips, "Bridging 'Town & Gown' Through Innovative University-Community Partnerships," *The Innovation Journal: The Public Sector Innovation Journal* 10, no. 2 (2005): 3.

2. John Dewey, *Experience and Education* (New York: Simon and Schuster, 2007), p. 46.

3. Martin, Smith, and Phillips, "Bridging 'Town & Gown'," p. 3.

4. Carnegie Foundation for the Advancement of Teaching, "Who We Are," accessed July 1, 2015, http://www.carnegiefoundation.org/who-we-are/.

5. Carnegie Foundation for the Advancement of Teaching, "The Carnegie Classification of Institutions of Higher Education," last modified July 1, 2015, http://carnegieclassifications.iu.edu.

6. Ira Harkavy and John L. Puckett, "Lessons from Hull House for Contemporary Urban Universities," *Social Service Review* 68, no. 3 (1994): 299–321.

7. Association of American Colleges and Universities, "A National Call to Action—A Crucible Moment: College Learning & Democracy's Future," accessed July 1, 2015, https://www.aacu.org/sites/default/files/files/crucible/Crucible_508F.pdf.

8. Carnegie Foundation for the Advancement of Teaching, "Carnegie Selects Colleges and Universities for 2015 Community Engagement Classification," accessed July 1, 2015, http://www.carnegiefoundation.org/newsroom/news-releases/carnegie-selects-colleges-universities-2015-community-engagement-classification/.

9. Florida International University, "Florida International University's World Ahead Strategic Plan 2010–2015," accessed July 1, 2015, http://stratplan.fiu.edu/docs/WorldsAhead_ StrategicPlan.pdf.

10. Susan Feinberg, "FIU Honors College Launches Innovative Community Partnership," *The Provost's Newsletter*, November 23, 2009, accessed July 15, 2015, http://news.fiu.edu/2009/ 11/fiu-honors-college-launches-innovative-community-partnership/7855.

11. This 15,000 figure is prior to the 2010 annexation of adjacent land. The City has now over 19,000 residents.

12. National Collegiate Honors Council, "What is Honors?" accessed May 28, 2014, http://nchchonors.org/public-press/what-is-honors/.

13. National Collegiate Honors Council, "Definition of Honors Education," accessed July 1, 2015, http://nchchonors.org/wp-content/uploads/2014/02/Definition-of-Honors-Education.pdf.

14. The 2014 report of the National Association of Colleges and Employers (NACE) for instance states that "employers made full-time offers to 64.8 percent of their interns." National Association of Colleges and Employers. "*2014 Internship & Co-op Survey—Executive Summary*," accessed July 1, 2015, http://www.naceweb.org/uploadedFiles/ Content /static-assets/downloads/executive-summary/2014-internship-co-op-survey-executive-summary.pdf.

15. National Collegiate Honors Council, "Honors Course Design," accessed July 1, 2015, http://nchchonors.org/faculty-directors/honors-course-design/.

16. Campus Compact, "Initiatives: Service-Learning," accessed July 1, 2015, http://www. compact.org/initiatives/ service-learning/.

17. CBR, defined as a "partnership of students, faculty, and community members who collaboratively engage in research with the purpose of solving a pressing community problem or effecting social change," is useful because it links academic knowledge and skills with action. It cannot, however, be fully developed and implemented within the structure of a class, even a one-year class, because the mutual

participation of residents cannot be obtained in such a short time frame. Service-research is therefore more appropriate. This definition comes from Kerry Strand et al., *Community-Based Research and Higher Education—Principles and Practices* (San Francisco: Jossey-Bass, 2003), p. 3.

18. Clifford Geertz, *The Interpretation of Cultures* (New York: Basics Books, 1973), p. 449.

19. Ibid., p. 436.

20. C.L.R. James, *Beyond a Boundary* (New York: Pantheon Books, 1993).

21. Elliott Gorn and Michael Oriard, "Taking Sports Seriously," *Chronicle of Higher Education* (March 24, 1995): A52.

22. Bernice Braid and Ada Long, Eds., *Places as Text: Approaches to Active Learning*. NCHC Monograph (Lincoln, NE: National Collegiate Honors Council, 2000), p. 71.

23. Ibid., p. 16.

24. Ibid., p. 24.

25. Ibid., p. 53.

26. Jerry W. Robinson Jr. and Gary Paul Green, Eds., *Introduction to Community Development—Theory, Practice, and Service-Learning* (Thousand Oaks, CA: Sage Publications, 2011), p. 256.

27. George Mariz, "The Culture of Honors," *Journal of National Collegiate Honors Council* 9, no. 1 (2008): 22.

28. Ibid., p. 23.

29. Ibid., p. 24.

30. Jim Ford, "Creating an Honors Culture," *Journal of National Collegiate Honors Council* 9, no. 1 (2008): 27–29, 28.

31. Deepening the Roots of Civic Engagement—2011 Annual Membership Survey—Executive Summary, Campus Compact, pp. 1–12, 10.

32. Ibid.

33. Florida International University. "Tiger Grants 2013," accessed July 1, 2015. http://cake.fiu.edu/TIGER2013/.

34. Jessica V. Barnes et al., "Creating and Sustaining Authentic Partnerships," *Journal of Higher Education and Engagement* 13, no. 4 (2009): 15–29, 16.

35. Strand et al., *Community-Based Research*, p. 28.

36. Ibid., p. xv.

37. Braid and Long, *Places as Text*, p. 70.

38. Even though money spent on programs launched in Sweetwater also benefits students, the Honors College cannot spend most of its funds because they are either state monies that cannot benefit an outside entity or donations that are earmarked for other uses. The Honors College cannot, for example, purchase 300 showerheads, even though it would benefit its students to organize a water conservation campaign and distribute free showerheads in the community.

39. For the 2014–2015 year, the Miami-Dade Public School Office charged about $99 per student for fingerprinting.

Chapter 3

Praxis Labs

Theory + Action as a Foundation of a Modern Honors Education

Sylvia Torti and Martha Bradley-Evans

In 2012, the Honors College at the University of Utah opened the Donna Garff Marriott Honors Residential Community, a place where academic, cocurricular, and living spaces concur. The building serves as a living space for over three hundred students and as a hub for 1,900 additional honors students. As students enter the building, whether they've just gotten off the nearby Trax commuter line, or have come back to the residence from elsewhere on campus, they pass a Utah sandstone rock with the motto "Serve the World," inviting them to reflect on the higher purpose of their education.

This residential community was designed to meet the needs of current and future honors students by embedding their experiences in a dynamic, physical place. Purposeful creation of physical communities is, and will continue to become, increasingly important to undergraduate education in a world that is globalized and virtualized, one in which students can sometimes exist without confronting the cultural and socioeconomic complexities of the world around them. The architecture and programming for the building were inspired by the ideals developed in Honors Praxis Labs, the topic of this chapter.

The motivation behind this residential community and Praxis Lab programming follows John Dewey's idea that the purpose of education is to develop the "capacity for associative living." As noted by Cecile Houry's chapter in this book, Dewey's vision assumes that democracy, education and citizenship are inextricably entwined, and that "democracy has to be born anew every generation and education is its midwife."[1] It assumes that there is an "organic connection between education and personal experience."[2] While easy to articulate and endorse, putting these lofty goals into practice is a common challenge faced by many honors programs.

The mission of the University of Utah's Honors College, consistent with Dewey's notion, is to help students become ethical and engaged citizens, empowering them to be problem solvers who positively impact the world around them. The program is committed to anchoring the undergraduate experience in a strong commitment to civic engagement, interdisciplinarity, and internationalization.[3] This commitment, however, is sometimes difficult to execute in an atmosphere where students bring heavily market-focused expectations to higher education.

Most students come to the university to prepare for careers, thinking primarily about financial wealth and professional stability—half of incoming honors students plan on becoming doctors, lawyers, or engineers—but many of them also hope for the personal satisfaction that comes with a commitment to public service.

Today's students have complex, constantly evolving relationships to politics, power, and civic engagement that don't always mirror those—either practiced or idealized—by faculty and administrators. National trends of pessimism and alienation voiced by students in the 1990s have given way to a new generation of students who are deeply motivated to engage their communities and want to make a positive difference in the world.[4]

According to the Pew Trust, today's students are "digital natives." For example, 81 percent of Millennials are on Facebook and their median friend count of 250 is far higher than that of older age groups.[5] They have seized the new digital platforms—the internet, mobile technology, social media—to construct personalized networks of friends, colleagues, and affinity groups. They are also part of an America that is more racially diverse than ever before. The Millennial generation is forging a distinctive path into adulthood. They are relatively unattached to organized politics and religion, linked by social media, burdened by debt, in no rush to marry—and optimistic about the future."[6]

Responding to these generational shifts in engagement, ethnic, cultural, and demographic shifts, is a challenge, and one that is uniquely suited to honors education, especially at large institutions. Traditional honors education, grounded in the liberal arts, has provided students with historical, cultural, and academic breadth, as well as disciplinary depth through completion of a thesis or capstone in their major.

This underpinning is no longer sufficient. In the process of completing undergraduate degrees, students should not view themselves simply as autonomous entrepreneurial consumers who are paying for credentials to find employment,[7] but they should leave the university with tangible workforce skills, a sense of social responsibility for the future vitality of their communities and the ability to negotiate the complexity that comes with civic engagement.

To achieve these goals, the University of Utah Honors College, in 2004, developed a new pedagogical model. Praxis Labs represent a version of community-based education that achieves these goals while connecting both residential and commuter students to campus and the community.[8]

Ideally, Praxis Labs are meant to instill in students a sustained desire to use their education in the production of public well-being, thereby nurturing a new generation of community leaders and creative problem solvers committed to cooperative thinking.

They provide a space for students to experience the uncertainty and risk that comes with moving new ideas and projects forward.

Unlike many service-learning courses, Praxis Labs vest the power and responsibility for project development, implementation, and outcomes with the students themselves.[9] Students must work as teams and develop their work within the context of relationships with one another, relationships that are built and evolve over the course.

The Praxis Lab model has the potential to become increasingly important in honors education because it translates the worth of a liberal arts honors education to students, institutions, and the community. This chapter provides an overview of the model, an analysis of a ten-year data set, including the strengths and challenges associated with Labs, and a discussion of how the model might be applied elsewhere.

SETTING AND HISTORY FOR THE DEVELOPMENT OF PRAXIS LABS

The University of Utah is an urban public university with 24,492 undergraduate students in fifteen colleges and professional schools and more than eighty majors. Eighty-seven percent of its students commute to campus, and 59 percent of them work twenty to thirty hours per week at paid jobs. Almost 50 percent of students transfer to the university after first studying at a community college or somewhere else.

The Honors College serves 2,200 students with an incoming honors class of 550 students per year. The opening of the Donna Garff Marriott Honors Community significantly increased the number of students living on campus, but still, 65 percent of honors students commute. Finding ways to connect a large student population at a predominantly commuter institution to a high quality liberal arts education, which flourishes best in close knit communities, is a key challenge.

Throughout the College's history, the primary avenue for connecting students was through honors Intellectual Traditions and honors writing courses—the types of classes one might find in any honors program.

These have been, and continue to serve as the core requirements of the honors bachelor's degree. However, additional efforts are necessary to deeply engage students.

In the late 1980s, with the development of the Campus Compact,[10] service-learning courses, giving students the chance to participate in community projects as part of course requirements, became common across the country. The University of Utah responded with the dedication of the Lowell Bennion Community Service Center in 1987, which began to engage honors students in meaningful nonacademic ways, but did not fully address or develop the intellectual curiosity, civic engagement, and creative problem-solving skills expected of honors students.

College leadership realized that honors students represented an immense reservoir of talent that could be, and should be, directed toward creative solutions to pressing contemporary problems. Leadership also felt that an honors education should prepare students to live in a rapidly changing internationalized world, to consider their roles as global citizens, to understand meaning in a diversity of ideas, of persons, of cultures, and of politics and how to work across these differences.

As described as necessary in *A Promising Connection*, Praxis Labs create the "facilitated opportunities for students to examine social, political, and organizational antecedents that reinforce inequities of power and privilege within communities which are key to civic engagement's educational potential."[11] The empowerment that comes with critical thinking in the context of community and global learning helps students discover how they might bring greater equity, fairness, and justice to local institutions and the global community.[12]

The Honors College launched its first Praxis Lab in the 2004–2005 academic year. "The Revitalization of Downtown Salt Lake City," with ten students and two professors, developed partnerships with the Downtown Alliance, the Redevelopment Agency, the Mayor's Office and eight other community organizations to create practical solutions for a dying downtown.

Students presented at three professional conferences, published a book of their findings for public dissemination and successfully lobbied for the term "Greek Town" to be placed on the light rail stop in the neighborhood they studied, which was originally settled by Greek organizations and the location of the current annual Greek Festival.

Community response to this new initiative was overwhelmingly positive, resulting in a demand for more Praxis Labs. Between 2005–2015, the Honors College has supported thirty unique Praxis Labs, and these Labs have included 369 students, sixty-six faculty members, and over twenty-three community partners (table 3.1).

Table 3.1 Summary of Praxis Labs 2005–2015

Praxis Lab Title	Discipline of Faculty	Community Partners	Specific Outcomes
Outcomes that Influence Power			
Transparency & Privacy in Digital World	Law	Salt Lake Tribune; Salt Lake City Corporation	Report of best practices for transparency in local governments. Creation of the Transparency Project: http://www.utahtransparencyproject.org/#!the-think-tank. Presentation to local mayors across state. Hosted a press conference. Formal resolution adopted by Salt Lake City Corporation
Wallace Stegner & Western Lands	Law, Writer/Photographer	Southern Wilderness Alliance, Grand County Commission	Comprehensive report delivered to legislators and environmental workers across state. Report cited five years later in bill proposal in Utah legislature
Middle Class on the Ropes	Sociologist, Economist	United Way, Salt Lake Community College	Hosted a community panel discussion for 150 people. Produced resource guide and narrative stories a la Studs Terkel
Air Quality, Health & Society	Atmospheric Scientist, Writer/Photographer	University of Utah Medical School, Breathe Utah	Presentation at Stegner Conference. Presentation of letter endorsed by business leaders to Governor. Creation of an animated white-board video in English and Spanish to teach about air quality to K3–5 graders
Revitalizing Downtown.	Architecture, Communication.	Downtown Alliance, RDA, Chamber of Commerce, Neighborworks.	Documentary film, research report, presentations at Vibrant Downtown Conference.
Outcomes that Positively Impact Underserved Populations			
Global Health	Public Health PhD, Infectious Disease MD	A village in Ghana, Refugee Services Organization	Creation of "Global Health Scholars"—an ongoing working group of 30 honors students/year
Planets & Pedagogy	Physics, Writer/Photographer	Rose Park Elementary School	Creation of a new honors course at K12 Title 1 school, which has resulted in increases in test scores

(*Continued*)

Table 3.1 Summary of Praxis Labs 2005–2015 (*Continued*)

Praxis Lab Title	Discipline of Faculty	Community Partners	Specific Outcomes
The Patient Experience	Architect/Design Professor, Medical Professionals	4th Street Health Clinic	Creation of non-profit, *Connect2Health*, that connects underserved populations to healthcare
Documentary Film and Diversity	Videographer, English/Creative Writer	Utah Humanities Council, University Neighborhood Partners	Creation of new honors course that brings adult learners with little previous access to higher education together with honors students to create documentary films
New American Communities	Sociologist, Community Activist	University Neighborhood Partners	
Social Change	Folklorist/Writer & Writer/Activist	Mestizo Arts Collective	Creation of "Social Justice" Scholars group
Empathetic Patient Experience	Architect/Designer, cancer professionals	Huntsman Cancer Institute	Restorative interactive herb gardens designed and built for patients of all abilities
Alzheimer's & Aging	MD/PhD, Composer & Ethnographer		Resource guide for families with members suffering dementia, five hundred copies distributed. Public events for patients and families designed and implemented across Salt Lake Valley
Westside Leadership Academy	Sociologist & Community Development	Neighborworks, University Neighborhood Partners	Documentary films
Community & Change	Sociologist & Activist, Community Organizer Economics & Education	University Neighborhood Partners	
Diversity and Education	Education Faculty	Salt Lake City School district; Utah State Legislators Hispanic Chamber of Commerce	Resource manual, distributed two thousand copies
			Film of testimonials of students in course
Quality of Life	Communication	Salt Lake Public Library	Design and implementation of "Pace of Life" conference at library
Environmental Health	MD & Economist		Healthy World, Health Home, Healthy You presentations to K12 students

Table 3.1 Summary of Praxis Labs 2005–2015 (Continued)

Praxis Lab Title	Discipline of Faculty	Community Partners	Specific Outcomes
Crossing the Religious Divide.	Episcopal Reverend & Baptist Pastor.	Eight local congregations including Catholic, Episcopalian, Latter-day Saint, Islamic, and Jewish	Design and implementation of two community-building dialogues for Salt Lake youth.

Outcomes that Positively Influence Campus

Praxis Lab Title	Discipline of Faculty	Community Partners	Specific Outcomes
Higher Education & Diversity	University President, AVP for Academic Affairs, VP for Business Administration	ASUU; Undergraduate Studies	Report proposing "best practices" for advising at the University of Utah
Ecosystem Services & the American Dream	Biologist, International Water Mediator	University of Utah, Department of Facilities and Office of Sustainability	Report analyzing water use on campus with recommendations to University administration for water conservation
Redefining Health & Wellness	MD physician, PhD nutritionist	Department of Nutrition	Created a new cooking course for nutrition minor with a cook book connecting recipes to the seven dimensions of health
Queer Identity & Social Justice	Sociologist, Social Worker	Gender Studies Program, Equality Utah	Creation of "SQARE" new student group for LGBTQ artists and activists on campus
Creativity on Center Stage (Education)	Historian, Dancer/ Choreographer	Stephen Brown Dance Company	Artistic production created and produced by students at Rose Wagner Theater
Uneasy Intersection of Law & Medicine	Philosopher, Judge, and Obstetrician	University of Utah Medical School	Design and presentation of curriculum for medical school to teach new doctors about pain killer abuse and post-prescription management
The Great Salt Lake	Film Director/ Producer, Ethnographer		Creative and Research Report
Energy & Sustainability	Biologist, City Planner	Metropolitan Planning Facilities and Planning, University of Utah	Creation of "Urban Ecology & Sustainability Scholars" group (ongoing group that works to implement more sustainable practices on campus)
The City as Laboratory.	Landscape Architect, City Planner.	None.	

PRAXIS LABS

In its simplest form, the Greek word praxis means theory plus action. Paulo Freire defined praxis as a "reflection and action upon the world in order to transform it."[13] In *The Human Condition,* Hannah Arendt used praxis to counter notions of "a contemplative life," a life that she judged as inadequate and incomplete.[14] According to Arendt, *praxis* is the highest level of active life and the true realization of human freedom and togetherness.[15] Praxis is a concept of participatory democracy that actively contrasts bureaucracy and elite politics because freedom in this sense means the "capacity to begin, to start something new, to do the unexpected."[16]

Praxis Labs, then, are a dynamic, participatory, democratic, and often transformative, honors education that should become an increasingly important core component in today's honors programs. The goal of Praxis Labs is to go beyond the material value of a degree and help students see ways in which they might use their education to address society's problems and to enrich their personal lives in the process.

As Arthur Levine and Jeannette Cureton point out, "Today's students need to believe they can make a difference. . . . But at the same time they are not convinced that they can both do good and do well."[17] Praxis Labs provide an opportunity to teach students they can do both by equipping them with the skills and encouragement to address issues head-on.

The Model

Each Praxis Lab is a year-long course built around a pressing social issue that usually falls into one of three broad categories: Energy/Environment, Health/Society, and Social Justice/Policy (table 3.1). The dean, in consultation with faculty and community members, choses complicated, current topics that cannot be solved by one discipline alone. Faculty expertise and their availability to lead, willing community partners, as well as student interest, also play a role in topic choice. Good topics are those that are global in scope but have a unique local manifestation.

The composition of course participants and course progression are also important. Each Praxis Lab engages two professors from different disciplines—experts from philosophers to physicians and from the campus to the community—and no more than twelve students, sophomore-senior. First year students have been included in the past, but generally their inclusion has not led to fruitful experiences for them or others.

During the fall semester, through readings, intense discussion and guest speakers, the faculty and students endeavor to understand the topic as fully as possible and to develop deeper expertise and empathy for all facets of the issue. By the end of the first semester, students define a particular aspect of the larger issue for which they will design and implement a solution in the local community.

The spring semester, then, is spent intensively designing, revising, implementing, and presenting the results of the project. Each class carries a $5,000 project budget and at the end of the year, in addition to honors elective credits, each student receives a $1,000 stipend. The project budget and stipend funds are drawn from funds raised privately through individual donors, corporations, or foundations.

As in all community-based research, Praxis Labs require students to work with people unlike themselves,[18] and this includes people who are culturally and socioeconomically diverse as well as students studying other majors. Unlike traditional community-based research, though, specific Praxis projects are identified not by the community partner or the faculty, but by the students.

This is an important distinction of the Praxis Lab model. Faculty and community partners largely relinquish their power to the students. Faculty do not have predefined products in mind and community partners do not task the Lab with specific projects they need to be completed. Instead, students are given the opportunity and the responsibility to define the problem based on the theory and input they've received from all stakeholders.

In the best scenarios, students respond purposefully to input from community partners and faculty, but ultimately, the decision about which project to work on lies with the students. This distinction is important because it requires students to take ownership, develop a cohesive problem as a group, and assume the risk associated with creating novel and viable solutions. These skills are not ordinarily practiced in their undergraduate studies.

Furthermore, these are not skills normally practiced by faculty or community partners. To allow students the freedom to decide for themselves, and to potentially "fail" to define and implement a meaningful project, is one of the most difficult tasks for Praxis leaders and partners.

Through Praxis Labs, students become co-creators of new knowledge and have the unique opportunity to connect action to theory. The efficacy of this approach has been documented in the work of Sarah Gallini and Barbara Moely:[19]

> Through academic praxis (application of theoretical concepts to action), students shift from being knowledge receivers to idea creators. Abstract concepts come into relief against the background of situation and context as students consider, apply, test, assess, and reevaluate multiple disciplinary approaches to solving an array of human, mechanical, and environmental challenges.

The experience with Praxis Labs at the University of Utah's Honors College concurs with Gallini and Moely's work. Student growth stems directly from the difficulty of applying abstract concepts to real problems. The value of this process cannot be overstated.

The Student Experience

Students are drawn to Labs largely because of the topics; in fact, 95 percent of students report they chose to participate because the topic appealed to them. In contrast, only 41 percent report the associated stipend influenced their decision, suggesting this model might be successful in programs and institutions without scholarship funds.

Students are drawn from a variety of majors. Over the past ten years, 369 students from seventy-three majors have participated in Praxis Labs, suggesting an average of five majors per Lab. The most popular majors of participating students are Political Science, History, English, Economics, Psychology, Chemistry, and Biology. Students from Communication, Sociology, Business, and Environmental Studies are somewhat common.

Engineering, Ballet and Modern Dance are rare because those students have heavily scripted schedules that leave little room for elective courses. That said, some of the most compelling responses about the impact of Praxis Labs have come from students in dance and engineering because the Lab provided them with a dramatic and important counterpoint to their major.

During September and October when students absorb, discuss, and complicate the material at hand, they are stretched intellectually and emotionally by a diversity of experts, conflicting studies, and diverse opinions. This stretching is key to the ability to learn how to think critically about multiple facets of an issue. As quoted by one student, "I have learned that there are no easy answers and more than likely, no absolutely right ones."[20]

After this early period, during late November or early December, students often experience a sort of crisis of identity and performance anxiety. The group knows they need to decide which aspect of the issue they will address and that they need to identify a specific project as well as create a plan for who will be responsible for various aspects. This is often a period of considerable ambiguity and is particularly painful for honors students who are so good at reading what professors expect them to do, how to get As, how to succeed, and how to out-perform others.

The ambiguity of the process teaches students a great deal because they are forced to navigate their way through that ambiguity. It is also an intangible outcome of this model that cannot be predetermined. Students struggle with being independent learners and with collaboration, often noting that the hardest part of a Praxis Lab is learning to listen, to not be reactive and to allow themselves and others to change their ideas. Finally, they point to being able to "agree to disagree" as a powerful experience.[21]

The most successful Praxis Labs are ones where students come together, struggle with multiple opinions on how to approach the problem and then develop a strategy for pushing ahead. Students reflect on what they are experiencing, and then finally achieve clarity in terms of focus, intent, design, and purpose.

To facilitate this process, a number of Labs in recent years have begun to incorporate a Feasibility, Impact, Sustainability, and Achievability (FISA) analysis to help students settle on a project. By giving each element of a project a FISA score, students hone their ideas and learn that sometimes, great ideas must be passed over because of time, expertise, or resource constraints. Learning a mechanism for making such decisions is a tool they carry beyond the Praxis Lab.

When asked to reflect on the Praxis Lab experience, students note they learn they cannot rely on powers of memorization or theory, but must do something that matters because there are "real people" involved.[22] Many students comment that the Praxis Lab experience was "life-changing" and that their largest growth area was learning to work in a group.[23]

In a comparison of all honors courses, Praxis Labs scored higher than all other courses, especially when looking at the overall effectiveness of the course and effectiveness of instructors.

The Faculty

The selection of faculty is much like match-making and perhaps the most important decision the dean makes in producing a Lab. Faculty should have advanced knowledge and passion for the subject matter, be willing to behave more like facilitators than traditional lectures, and they should believe in the open-ended enterprise. Faculty develop the core concept, identify essential readings, invite guest speakers, prepare for additional activities (e.g., field trips) and connect with community partners. In many cases, faculty are recruited because of their existing relationship with community partners.

Ideal faculty members are committed to reciprocal-learning—learning that moves in both directions within and outside the classroom and with partners in community situations. They also should be adept at creating environments where reciprocal-learning is valued and respected. Rather than the hierarchical space of a traditional lecture hall, this type of collaborative learning, research, and creative problem-solving is produced around a table, in a circle of chairs, and sometimes on the lawn.

Praxis faculty must model collaborative behavior: how two individuals from different disciplinary backgrounds engage in intellectual discourse, make decisions, and work together toward creative solutions. When there is a power differential between the faculty, one is an established professor and one is a new adjunct for example, there can be one who leads and one who fades into the background. If this important partnership is out of balance or isn't working well, it casts a pall over the experience more broadly.

Most faculty who lead Praxis Labs have not worked together before. The best teams have a type of chemistry that bypasses differences, lack of common history, or experience in working as partners. As has been the case for two or three Praxis Labs, sometimes the matches don't work and the faculty fail to connect with one another, catch the rhythm of the class, the group dynamic, the importance of the collaborative teaching style or the enterprise itself.

Praxis faculty comment that they learn a great deal about themselves as individuals and teachers through the process: when to step forward or when to let the students lead out, how to let the discussions flow, how to help students form the central project question, or how to have the trust to let group dynamics evolve with a natural rhythm rather than being overly directorial and shaping it themselves.

Although the successful marriage that comes about through faculty selection need only last one year, 92 percent of the faculty surveyed reported that teaching the Praxis Lab resulted in long-lasting professional collaborations with co-faculty, which helps to drive interdisciplinary work on campus.

The Community Partners

Community partners are critically important. Partners are chosen because they are engaged in work around the topic and have insights, hopes, and frustrations that are based in the real world. Sometimes partners are chosen early by the dean and/or faculty because of existing relationships, and in this case, they contribute to the overall topic development (e.g., Bridging the Religious Divide, Westside Leadership Institute, New American Communities, Transparency and Privacy in a Digital World, etc.). In other cases, partnerships develop during the course of the fall semester as students hear from experts and multiple community organizations that speak to the issue (e.g., Wasatch Water, Empathetic Patient Experience, Planets and Pedagogy).

Always, partners help students see the distance between theory and application, which is sometimes fraught with obstacles, challenges, and mishaps. They share how they get things done in the context of the community, within a legal framework, or with limited resources, and in the process they make the issues come alive in all their real-world dimensions.

Research on the impact of civic engagement pedagogies suggests "that the primary cognitive task of college is not simple content mastery (the traditional focus of most courses) but, rather, meaningful engagement with content that facilitates development of complex moral judgments and understanding of self as part of larger social contexts."[24] For the Praxis model to be successful, community partners must agree that the enterprise is largely process-oriented and geared toward student education. They must understand students are smart, passionate, and idealistic, but not likely to have had experience putting ideas into action. Deliverable products are an expectation, but everyone accepts the risk that is inherent with student-run work.

It is incumbent on the dean and faculty to ensure that community partners understand this model. Fortunately, the University of Utah has two solid organizations on and off campus (i.e., Bennion Center and University Neighborhood Partners) with established liaisons to the broader community that have played an important role in helping to connect Praxis Labs to the community.

LEARNING OUTCOMES AND ASSESSMENT

Praxis Labs have measureable and immeasurable outcomes for individual students, faculty and the community. The overall learning goal is for students to experience intellectual growth through interdisciplinary thinking and engagement with complicated, pressing social issues, thereby illuminating and expanding on what they have learned in more traditional courses. This is one of the few times, in an otherwise scripted undergraduate education, in which they practice skills they will need to successfully contribute to future organizations.

Specifically, the Labs are designed to help students: evaluate complicated issues from the perspective of their disciplines, and then examine the same issue from the perspective of other disciplines; understand the complexity of collaborative project development and implementation under a deadline that includes multiple stakeholders; experience the excitement and discomfort associated with risk-taking and uncertainty of success; practice summarizing, writing, and communicating through the production of a well-edited written report; learn the art of presentation and practice speaking to diverse audiences across campus and in the community; build a sense of belonging, responsibility and confidence in their ability to effect change.

The learning outcomes are assessed qualitatively including self-evaluations, personal narratives, faculty evaluations, and a general assessment of project worth by the dean/community, though there is still work to be done to better understand the short- and long-term learning outcomes of this model. A database is being developed to follow student success, career choices, and long-term reflection after graduation.

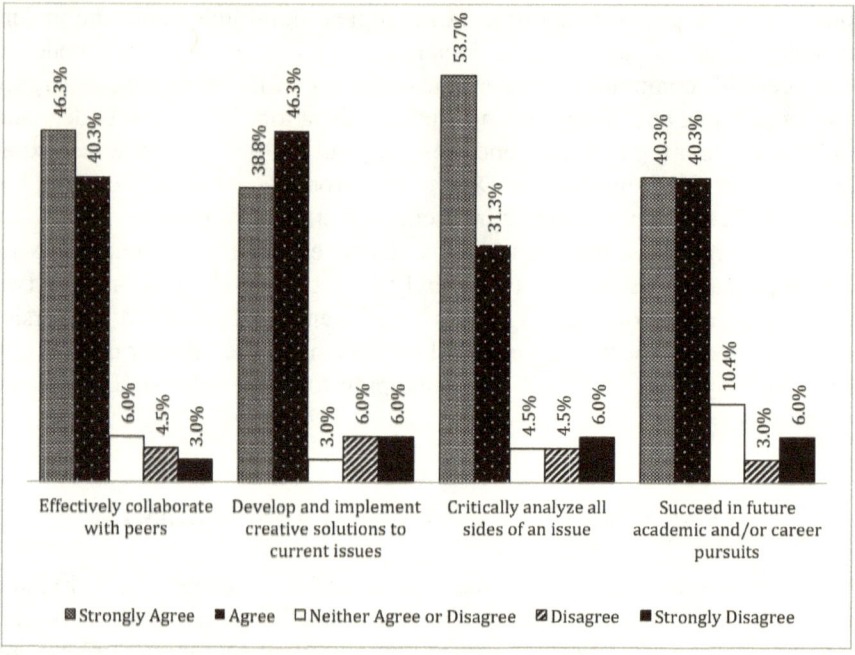

Figure 3.1 Student self-assessment of learning outcomes. *Source*: Honors College Praxis Lab Student Survey, October 4, 2013.

Figure 3.2 Student self-assessment of transformational nature of experience. *Source*: Honors College Praxis Lab Student Survey, October 4, 2013.

The majority of students that the skills they learned were extremely valuable for intellectual and emotional growth as well as marketability after college (figure 3.1) and 73.1 percent report that the experience was transformational (figure 3.2).

Faculty Impacts

Praxis Labs have a positive effect on faculty development; 92 percent of the faculty report that leading a Praxis Lab was a highly rewarding experience. When asked to elaborate on the positive nature of the experience, faculty say that they benefited because the increased student autonomy in Labs resulted in more engaged students. They also valued the close, extended collaboration with students and said that it was inspirational to see student growth through the course.

They also learn about themselves as professionals as expressed by Dr. Kevin Perry who co-led a Praxis Lab on Air Quality, Health, and Society:

> The class had a profound impact on me as an instructor. Prior to the class my research focused on societally relevant air quality issues. I conducted the research, compiled the results, presented my findings to the funding or regulatory agency and let them figure out what to do with the information. I have learned that it is possible to simultaneously advocate for improved air quality without jeopardizing my scientific reputation and my academic career. For me, that was a very unexpected result of participating in the Praxis Lab.

Many Praxis faculty members experience this kind of transformation as professionals, and make new connections between their professional and personal lives, an outcome that Dewey, Arendt, and Freire would surely endorse.

Praxis Labs also offer faculty a space in which they can experiment with new pedagogies that can later be taken back their regular teaching assignments. Seventy-six percent reported that Praxis Labs "allow me to try new pedagogical techniques that I can use in my regular teaching/professional work." In this way, the Honors College functions not only to educate students, but as an important laboratory for university faculty where they can try new teaching pedagogies, explore new collaborations, and work in an interdisciplinary space.

Products and Outcomes

Outcomes over the past ten years can be organized into three broad categories, those that positively influence power disparities, those that positively impact underserved populations, and those that positively influence campus (table 3.1).

Examples of Praxis Labs that have taken on sociopolitical power structures include: Transparency and Privacy in the Digital Age, Immigration, Wallace Stegner and Western Lands, and Air Quality, Health and Society. In Transparency and Privacy in the Digital Age, students entered the national conversation about transparency around WikiLeaks by researching transparency in Utah's cities and counties. They drafted a "best practices" manifesto for transparency in local governments and presented these at a student organized press conference. Later that year, their recommendations were formally adopted by Salt Lake City Corporation.

In Wallace Stegner and Western Lands, students created a report on Canyonlands National Park and published their work in the *Journal of the Hinckley Institute*. The report was used five years later as key supporting documentation for a proposed bill to enlarge the park. State senators invited students still in town to participate in the press conference announcing the proposed bill at the state capitol.

Students in Immigration wrote a primer on Utah's immigration history, including information on legislation, data on the economic impacts of immigrants, personal narratives and diversity of community agencies working around this issue. More than two thousand copies were circulated to teachers, counselors, principals, state legislators, and community groups. Seven years later, the resource guide continues to be used locally in discussions of immigration.

Many Praxis Labs have focused on work that influences or positively impacts underserved populations (table 3.1). For example, students in the Pedagogy and Planets worked with scientists, teachers and a Title I school to design a sixth grade curriculum that uses astronomy to teach science. At the end of the Lab, a local foundation agreed to fund an ongoing honors course to teach the curriculum and the course has been offered every fall with optional paid internships for students in the spring. As the principal of the school attests, both honors students and the Title I school continue to benefit from the relationship:

> Rose Park had the most growth in science literacy of any Title I elementary school in the district.... I believe that our success was in large part to our partnership with the Honors College.[25]

Clearly, the impact of one Praxis Lab can, with the right partners and funding, have ongoing, compounded effects on local partners.

One Praxis Lab, The Patient Experience, used design thinking to create a student-run program to improve the well-being of underserved community members by connecting them to, and helping them utilize, existing resources. The program resulted in the creation of a highly successful nonprofit (Connect2Health), which brings university students to work at health clinics that serve uninsured, often homeless, patients. With further charitable donations, Connect2Health has been expanded to three additional clinics, serving over a thousand patients with forty-five student volunteers and in 2015 secured AmeriCorps support.

Finally, Praxis Labs go beyond positively impacting campus and create new sustainable programs. Eight Praxis Labs have resulted in new curricula, thereby broadening the scope and benefit of the work to subsequent cohorts. Other Labs have resulted in changes in policy, campus climate or new working groups (e.g., Energy and Sustainability, Wasatch Water and the American Dream, Community and Change, Global Health). Finally, Labs have taken on themes that are socially relevant (e.g., Queer Identity), providing learning spaces that help to define the college as an inclusive and socially progressive space.

Successes and Challenges

There are Praxis Labs that were inspired, transformative and resulted in tangible and intangible results, and there have been Praxis Labs that failed. Praxis Labs didn't work when one of the co-instructors could not adjust to the nonhierarchical, collaborative, community-based teaching and learning style. Other times, faculty failed to help students focus, tie down an idea and clearly articulate goals early enough in the second semester to leave time for development and implementation. Sometimes students have taken on individual projects rather than a single group project, thereby failing to work as a collaborative team.

There is a sort of magic in a successful Praxis Lab that is difficult to quantify. A perfectly chosen topic helps, but the faculty selected to lead the group are also key, as are the community partners.

Ultimately, a successful Praxis Lab is grounded in trust. Students must trust the faculty to guide them through unfamiliar territory—learning to trust their instincts, abilities, and creative ideas. Community partners must trust students and faculty to hear the way they experience the world and its problems. Faculty must trust one another and be comfortable with student anxiety around ambiguity so that they do not step in and dictate solutions. They must also trust students and their untested abilities to muddle through to thoughtful, active solutions.

Funding Barriers

There are significant obstacles to interdisciplinary work that play out in the Praxis Lab. The first is the funding model. Praxis Labs typically have two instructors rather than one, a project budget, student stipends, and are capped at twelve students. All of these are critical elements that enrich the classroom experience, lend a sort of freedom or experimental quality to the class, encourage students to take risks, and make it possible for students to opt to participate in a Praxis Lab rather than something else.

Faculty salaries can usually be covered by the base budget, but the rest of the funds come from development activity. Working to fund Praxis Labs with endowment funds is a long-term goal, but in the interim and for the past ten years, community partners—foundations, individual donors and in some cases, companies—have funded this important civic engagement activity.

Praxis Labs also take personnel time and are often started one or two years before the Lab. The dean or director must have the time to research faculty, spend time in the match-making phase, clearly explain the model and then set expectations adequately. He or she must be well connected on campus and in the community, able to choose a topic that is timely, and able to motivate others. In a typical year, the honors dean spends four to five hours a week connecting with the constituent groups in current Labs, discussing future topics with faculty, students and community members, and raising funds.

Student Barriers

A second challenge is integrating this curriculum with other university requirements. Honors students tend to be practical and focused on graduation and don't always see the value of elective credit. Furthermore, students don't naturally embrace the value of risk and ambiguity and must be mentored on how to negotiate their performance anxiety in this context. They don't intuitively know that communication, reasoning, empathy, tolerance, non-routine problem-solving, creative thinking, and collaboration, as well as how to optimize project development and implementation, are skills that must be practiced again and again before one becomes proficient.

Another ongoing issue is one about pacing, life balance, and time management. Praxis Labs have been described as "greedy beasts." Students and faculty become so engrossed in the work, in the relationships, the power of the collaboration and community that they would prefer to do it only and perhaps neglect everything else. Again, these difficulties can become incredibly powerful learning moments that generate reflection, planning, and group interaction that will impact the way students engage in meaningful work in the future.

TRANSFERABILITY OF MODEL AND
FUTURE OF HONORS EDUCATION

Students need both the foundations of a liberal arts education and a space where they can engage the big issues of their times—energy, the environment, health care, social change, globalization—in ways that teach them practical skills and intangible life-lessons in empathy and civic engagement.

As John Seely Brown states, "It's never enough to just tell people about some new insight. Rather, you have to get them to experience it in a way that evokes its power and possibility. Instead of pouring knowledge into people's head, you need to help them grind a new set of eyeglasses so they can see the world in a new way."[26]

For students, community partners and faculty alike, the Praxis Lab creates an environment where risk-taking is valued and integral, where student work has a real-world application, and where the university is responsive and connected to the community.

Praxis Labs should be transferable to other research-based institutions or liberal arts colleges with access to a nearby, noncollege community. The Labs could work at two-year honors programs at research universities or community colleges as a capstone experience to be taken in year two, although in our experience having students of different ages/years is an asset.

Another model might be to connect a Praxis Lab at a four-year institution with a seminar at a two-year college. During Middle Class on the Ropes, a faculty member at Salt Lake Community College participated in early discussions about the Lab and then created writing assignments in her own seminar around this topic. This is a connection that could be built upon in future years and could be highly fruitful for students and faculty at both institutions.

Educators must find ways to embrace the ambiguity inherent in the Praxis Lab model in education because regardless of topic, faculty, or particular student population, these experiences mirror the real world where individuals are asked to be nimble, flexible, and resourceful to creatively address common contemporary issues.

In his book, *Civic Provocations,* David Scobey writes about the evolving nature of higher education in the twenty-first century with regard to the types of degrees and disciplines, the organizational structures of university, and funding models. As he says, "The question is not whether the academy will be changed, but how."[27]

A half a century ago, in 1947, Martin Luther King articulated his vision for higher education by focusing on the changed mind that should result:

> Education must also train one for quick, resolute and effective thinking. To think incisively and to think for one's self is very difficult. We are prone to let our mental life become invaded by legions of half truths, prejudices, and propaganda. Education must enable one to sift and weigh evidence, to discern the true from the false, the real from the unreal, and the facts from the fiction. The function of education, therefore, is to teach one to think intensively and to think critically.[28]

Despite the changing world stage that students confront in the twenty-first century, the core mission of higher education is still to provide the intellectual and pedagogical context for the "changed mind," a mind with fine-tuned critical reading, writing, and communication skills, with a developed social conscience, the ethical and moral tools for informed citizenship, and a preparation for empathetic involvement as members of communities and the global environment.

A great power in the Praxis Lab model is in the intimacy of the relationships—between peers, between students and faculty, and those individuals with the community. Theory is not only put into action, praxis in the truest sense, but it is made personal. This personal aspect is extremely important in an era marked by an increased dependency on technology, the increased distance of "virtual" social space, and the breakneck speed with which information is shared. Developing common currency in skills at creative problem-solving, effective collaboration, and the ability to form relationships with persons who are different from oneself, are of new importance.

Praxis Labs assume honors students will become effective, empathetic, and creative contributors to their communities. In addition to the hard skills mentioned above, students will see the way theory and action can help them address the most pressing issues of their times, both those that stem from the collective environments they have inherited as well as those they will experience through their own creation.

This well-structured, but open-ended community-based honors curriculum, provides students with the skills and confidence that they can individually and collectively, in small but significant ways, have an impact on the world in which they live. Thus, Honors Praxis Labs bring us closer to the ideal of an integrated undergraduate education so critical to the citizenry of the twenty-first century.

KEY IDEAS IN THIS CHAPTER

- Higher education, and honors colleges in particular, need to devote greater focus to the practical skills and sense of personal responsibility that their students gain as a result of their educational experience.
- Praxis Labs are an innovative and experiential pedagogy where students, faculty, and community partners share ownership over the questions engaged in the class and move from "theory to practice" as they consider and attempt to positively impact concrete, real-world problems.
- Such efforts involve challenges and are not for every student, faculty member, or community partner but the experience of Praxis Labs at the University of Utah suggests numerous positive outcomes that can be reaped when such innovations are approached systematically and intentionally.

NOTES

1. Janet Eyler and Dwight E. Giles, *Where's the Learning in Service Learning* (San Francisco: Jossey-Bass, 1999), p. 154.
2. John Dewey, *Experience and Education* (New York: Macmillan Press, 1938).
3. University of Utah President David Pershing, inauguration address, October 2012.
4. Elizabeth Hollander and Matthew Hartley, "Reimagining the Civic Imperative of Higher Education," in *A Different Kind of Politics: Readings on the Role of Higher Education in Democracy*, Ed. D. Barker and D. W. Brown (Dayton, Ohio: Kettering Foundation, 2009), pp. 1–14; Peter Levine, *Agent of Democracy: Higher Education and the HEX Journal*, Ed. David W. Brown and Deborah Witte (Dayton, Ohio: Kettering Foundation Press, 2008), p. 18.
5. Pew Research Center, "Millennials in Adulthood: Detached from Institutions, Networked with Friends," March 7, 2014, accessed July 15, 2015, http://www.pewsocialtrends.org/2014/03/07/millenials-in-adulthood/.
6. Ibid.
7. David Hursh and Andrew F. Wall, "Re-politicizing Higher Education and Research within Neoliberal Globalization," *Policy Futures in Higher Education* 9, no. 5 (2011): 560–572.
8. Margaret Zamudio, Francisco Rios and Angela M. Jaime, "Thinking Critically about Difference: Analytical Tools for the 21st Century," *Equity and Excellence in Education* 41, no. 2 (2005): 215–229.
9. Kerry Strand et al., *Community-Based Research and Higher Education: Principles and Practices* (San Francisco: Jossey-Bass, 2003), p. 20.
10. Campus Compact. "Building Engaged Campuses," accessed July 18, 2015, http://www.compact.org/wp-content/uploads/resources/downloads/Retention_Research_Brief.pdf.
11. Christine M. Cress, Cathy Burack, Dwight E. Giles, Jr., Julie Elkins, and Margaret C. Stevens, *A Promising Connection: Increasing College Access and Success through Civic Engagement* (Boston: Campus Compact, 2010).
12. Martha Nussbaum, "The Liberal Arts Are Not Elitist," *Chronicle of Higher Education*, February 28, 2010, accessed June 10, 2015, http://chronicle.com/article/The-Liberal-Arts-Are-Not/64355/; Lee Knefelkamp, "Civic Identity: Locating Self in Community," *Diversity and Democracy* 11, no. 3 (2008): 1–3; Anne Colby and William M. Sullivan, "Strengthening the Foundations of Students' Excellence, Integrity and Social Contribution," *Liberal Education* 95, no. 1 (2009): 22–29.
13. Paolo Freire, *Pedagogy of the Oppressed* (New York: Herder and Herder, 1970), 33.
14. Hannah Arendt, *The Human Condition*, 2nd edition. Chicago: University of Chicago Press, 1998.
15. Stanford Encyclopedia of Philosophy, "Hannah Arendt," accessed July 13, 2015, http://plato.stanford.edu/entries/arendt/.
16. Strand et al., *Community-Based Research,* p. 123, 134.
17. Arthur Levine and Jeannette Cureton, *When Hope and Fear Collide: A Portrait of Today's College Students* (San Francisco: Jossey-Bass, 1999), p. 187.

18. Strand et al., *Community-Based Research*, p. 146.

19. Sarah Gallini and Barbara Moely, "Service-Learning and Engagement, Academic Challenge, and Retention," *Michigan Journal of Community Service Learning* 10, no. 1 (2003): 5–14.

20. Participant in Wallace Stegner and Western Lands.

21. Participant in Immigration.

22. Participant in Revitalizing Downtown.

23. Participant in Community and Change.

24. Lynn E. Swaner, "Educating for Personal and Social Responsibility: A Review of the Literature," *Liberal Education Review* 92, no. 3 (2005): 14.

25. Nicole Warren (Principal of Rose Park Elementary School), personal communication with author, July 2015.

26. John Seely Brown, *Seeing Differently: Insights on Innovation* (Boston: Harvard Business Press, 1997), p. 245.

27. David Scobey, "Why now? Because this is a Copernican Moment," in *Civic Provocations: Bringing Theory to Practice*, Ed. Donald Harward (Washington, DC: Association of American Colleges and Universities, 2012), pp. 13–18.

28. Martin Luther King Jr., "The Purpose Of Education," accessed July 16, 2015, http://www.drmartinlutherkingjr.com/thepurposeofeducation.htm.

Chapter 4

The "College" as an Emergent Global Form

One Experience at Starting a Transnational College-to-College Relationship

Catelijne Coopmans, Gregory Clancey,
and François G. Amar

Bilateral relationships between educational programs in different parts of the world are an increasingly popular goal, yet hard to initiate and sustain. While individual faculty and students move easily between distant campuses on visiting fellowships and exchanges, often leading to profound transformations in their scholarly and personal trajectories, it is less clear how bilateral relations at the institutional level can be transformative. How are programs to come together in a more than a ceremonial or superficial way, and why should they want to?

This chapter describes a geographically ambitious yet self-consciously informal attempt by two colleges—a long-established American honors college and a newly founded Singaporean residential college teaching a general education curriculum—to learn from one another's programs in a way that others might emulate. This comes at a moment of renewed worldwide interest in the creation of learning communities that personalize undergraduate education in large research universities.[1]

Traditionally associated with American, British, and (formerly British) Commonwealth universities, colleges within universities are beginning to be established in Asia and elsewhere, indicating that this old model is continuing to speciate, and in so doing, is becoming truly global for the first time.[2] Many American honors programs also operate as colleges, but, as this chapter goes to print, few have taken advantage of the opportunity for international college-to-college relationships.

No matter how varied colleges in different systems and traditions may be, they are often more similar to each other than they are to the programs, departments, and institutes that surround them at the research universities of which they are part. As relationships between relatively small-scale and intimate learning communities, college-to-college ties have the potential to enrich the honors experience in the same manner transnational departmental and university-level relationships provide "added value" for students and staff.

For such ties to emerge, progressive American honors programs of the future must reach out to their overseas counterparts even if the word "honors" is often not well recognized beyond the American shoreline. The word "college" certainly is, and this provides a firm basis for honors programs to find and interact with similar communities abroad.

A WORLD OF COLLEGES

The term "college" is very old, and refers to various types of institutions. For example, Americans commonly use the word to describe what in Singapore, the United Kingdom, and many other countries would be called a "faculty."[3] For the purposes of this chapter, the term "college" is used to refer to self-described undergraduate colleges within research universities which have a multidisciplinary if not transdisciplinary character and/or mission.

Some colleges are residential and some offer teaching, or at least tutoring. Many have their own building(s), staff, and students. Colleges typically have a carefully cultivated sense of community which is rare in academic departments and nearly impossible to achieve in the research university as a whole.

Some universities organize all or nearly all their students into colleges and are said to have "collegiate systems." Universities which have full or nearly full collegiate systems are found mainly in the United Kingdom and in (formerly British) Commonwealth countries. Collegiate systems also exist at a few American universities, such as Yale, Harvard, and Rice, who closely emulate the British model.

With the exception of Oxbridge, colleges under this system tend to emphasize residential living and pastoral care, leaving most teaching to departments. By contrast, the "honors college" is an American innovation. Honors colleges are nearly always teaching colleges, which may or may not have a residential component to their community structure.

The American and Commonwealth colleges have more recently been joined by a variety of hybrid models such as the one discussed below at the National University of Singapore (NUS). This development makes it possible to identify an emergent "collegiate way" with manifestations not only in North America and Europe, but in South Africa, Australia, Singapore, Macau, Hong Kong, India, Korea, Japan, Thailand, the Persian Gulf states, and elsewhere.

The organization of an international "Collegiate Way" Conference at Durham University in 2014, and the ongoing planning for a second such conference at the Australian National University in 2016 has created one of the first platforms for a coming-together of these diverse college models.[4] Notably absent from the Durham Conference, however, were American honors colleges, perhaps due to the organizers' emphasis on "collegiate systems," which are more common elsewhere.

While American honors colleges have their own domestic conferences—chiefly the National Collegiate Honors Council Conference, and the (newer) Honors Education at Research Universities conference—leaving them out of the global mix risks provincializing that model. In turn, this risks ignoring potential connections and shared interests between people who live and work in colleges globally.

The international emergence of colleges is bound up with the latent recognition that they have a role to play in the reputations of their universities abroad. With few exceptions, universities have long perceived their own colleges or college systems as localisms, related as they usually are to the education and development of undergraduates and lacking an explicit research function. In global branding, universities normally present themselves externally with a research-oriented vocabulary like "cutting-edge," "innovative," and "award-winning."

Colleges have been positively categorized as pastoral, nurturing, intimate, and exclusive—all of which they are—but not as markers of how universities project their charisma and reputation in global competition. The challenge for colleges in the twenty-first century is to demonstrate to their university patrons that this is a false dichotomy. A place to begin is with greater awareness of their global speciation and the reasons behind this trend.

A TRANS-GLOBAL CONNECTION

The Honors College of the University of Maine ("UM Honors") and Tembusu College of the National University of Singapore ("Tembusu") would at first glance seem unlikely partners for a bilateral relationship. They are about as far apart geographically as two places can be, and in parts of the world with few preexisting connections beyond English as a common language. Singapore is an urban, highly planned society with people of multiple ethnicities and religions living in close proximity, while Maine is rural and mostly Caucasian, with some influence of French and Native American cultures.

UM Honors displays many aspects of the "fully developed" American model as outlined by the National Collegiate Honors Council.[5] Tembusu, named after a native tree, is a new institution offering a small set of general education courses within a Commonwealth-inspired university curriculum.

Yet these colleges have much in common, as the Dean of the UM Honors College and the Master of Tembusu found when a chance meeting marked the start of an ongoing connection.

A first commonality is that both colleges help students fulfill general education core requirements in distinctive ways, compared to the universities in which they are embedded. Small seminar-style classes are hallmarks of both colleges. These seminars exist alongside, and bring together students from, many different degree programs in the two universities. While the colleges achieve multidisciplinarity in their mix of both staff and students, the topical focus of many classes transcends discipline-based learning altogether.

Beyond the basic curriculum, each college environment provides students with individualized opportunities for professional and personal development. These include the chance to work with faculty members on projects of mutual interest, which may be research focused, concerned with life at the college, or aimed at connecting with communities beyond.

A second commonality is that the two colleges are sources of pride and cultural capital for their respective universities. Tembusu and its neighboring colleges[6] are part of the architecturally striking campus-extension called University Town, feature prominently in university literature, and have become the regular focus of VIP tours for visitors to NUS. Likewise, UM Honors was recently recognized as one of the University of Maine's "Signature Programs," the only purely undergraduate teaching program to be so designated alongside six highly regarded research centers and areas of excellence.

A third commonality is that local rather than international students constitute the vast majority of members at each college: Singaporeans in the case of Tembusu and students from Maine and New England in the case of UM Honors.[7] This is a function of both being embedded in large publicly-funded universities whose mission is first to serve their own citizenry.

In line with this, the University of Maine and the National University of Singapore charge tuition differentially, so local students pay substantially less than those from abroad (or, in Maine's case, "out of state"). Colleges at public universities around the world are likely in the same situation of first needing to extend their substantial benefits to local students and only secondarily to those from elsewhere.[8]

Given this focus on offering an enhanced educational experience to a select group of mostly local undergraduates, the adoption of an international outlook—expressed in Tembusu's and UM Honors' interest in collaborating—may not seem an obvious direction for colleges. Nor do parent universities typically assign their colleges such a role, except perhaps when it comes to cultivating overseas alumni.

International exposure for undergraduates is certainly valued by the University of Maine and the National University of Singapore, both of which have made extensive investments in exchange programs with foreign partner universities, though not yet with one another. Yet there is no clearly laid out path for colleges such as Tembusu and UM Honors to directly partake in such exchange programs, which are normally the province of departments and not of colleges that facilitate only a small portion (at least in quantitative terms) of a student's undergraduate education.

Encouraged by their similarities and interested in fostering ties, yet realizing the absence of a clear path, the two colleges decided to start searching for opportunities "outside the box." They began with ad hoc exchanges of students and faculty for short-term intensive summer courses and visits. A fellow at Tembusu spent a month at UM Honors to teach a summer course in 2014. In the same summer, two students from UM Honors went to Tembusu for an intensive three-week course titled *Asia Now! The Archaeology of the Future City*.

These travel exchanges continued into a second academic year. In October 2014, another Tembusu faculty member, visited the UM Honors College and participated in UMaine's Climate Change Institute's Climate Adaptation and Sustainability Conference. In 2015, the Dean of UM Honors was invited as a Visiting Fellow to Tembusu, and a Tembusu faculty member was likewise invited to Maine as a Visiting Scholar, neither with the requirement that they teach.

As of the time of publication, the colleges are planning their first sabbatical exchange, and are discussing how to connect students in parallel courses through projects and online discussion. All of this has been done without a formal Memorandum of Understanding, with no special request of resources from their respective universities, and with minimal impacts on respective college budgets. And yet over the course of only two years the two colleges have got to know each other well, both as institutions and collections of individuals.

THE "ASIAN CENTURY"?

Given the positioning of this book predominantly for a U.S. audience, it may be far from obvious why an honors college in Maine should be concerned with Asia. Europe, Africa, and the Middle East still loom much larger in the consciousness of most East Coast American universities, even as Asia's economic importance in the world continues to rise, and Asian countries such as China, India, South Korea, and Singapore invest more heavily than the rest of the world in higher education.

One aim of this section then is to put these developments in Asia on the radar of faculty and administrators who are involved in honors programs and colleges in the United States. Universities in the United States (and the University of Maine is no exception) are currently cultivating Asia and especially China as potential sources for fee-paying students. While this is natural and positive for all concerned, engagement with this half of the world should extend more deeply, and college-to-college relationships offer a unique opportunity to do so.

The recent move to establish living-and-learning colleges at the National University of Singapore can be attributed to a confluence of pressures and trends. Among these is a concern with the economic competitiveness of both graduates and of the education sector itself. Another aspect is the aspiration of an increasingly affluent and assertive middle class, which is no longer content with the tightly discipline-based degree structure that was a feature of state developmental models. The American liberal arts college model is increasingly attractive in this part of the world even as its relevance is seemingly called into question at its point of origin.

Moreover, Singapore wishes to be an educational hub for Asia: a place that offers the type and quality of education desired by its own population and that also attracts the best and the brightest students from countries such as China, India, Malaysia, Indonesia, Thailand, and Vietnam.[9] Educational innovation and differentiation are part of this mission.

Through partnerships with foreign universities since the late 1990s, Singapore has consolidated its historical educational ties to the United States, the United Kingdom, Australia, and also China.[10] For example, the National University of Singapore has partnered with Duke to set up Singapore's first graduate medical school, and with Yale to establish its first liberal arts college (Yale-NUS, a close neighbor of Tembusu). The new Singapore University of Technology and Design has links to MIT and to Zheijang University, while Nanyang Technological University's new medical school is a collaboration with Imperial College London.

These influences have created variety and competition in the higher education sector. A greater space for multi- and interdisciplinarity and for the liberal arts has also opened up. In public discourse, these developments are explained (and public spending on them justified) predominantly on the basis of their value in helping to prepare graduates for a changing local and global labor market. This stays close to the belief that education is "training for the economy, an approach that is historically rooted in the country's postcolonial determination to succeed as a nation against the odds."[11]

A 2010 speech by the president of the National University of Singapore, Tan Chorh Chuan, illustrates this connection:

> Presently, many Asian universities still use education models with a high degree of specialised education. It is critical, however, for education to become much

more broad based and multidisciplinary. This is because most of the graduates of the future will need to be prepared for a "lifetime of careers," and not a "career for life." Data from the US Department of Labour indicated that an average person with a US college degree had 10 jobs between the ages of 18 to 42, with two-thirds of the jobs held before 27. These jobs may be in completely different sectors. The graduates of the future must also be able to deal with complex issues that cross many domains of knowledge. To equip graduates to be able to take on many jobs in different industry sectors, and to deal effectively with complexity, universities must adopt more broad-based education models.[12]

While specialized education leading to domain-specific expertise is still highly valued, there is an increasingly strong call for university education to offer students opportunities to engage beyond disciplines and develop as self-motivated, adaptive learners.

These reforms are not about simply importing "Western" models of education. University leaders in Singapore have adapted such models to suit twenty-first-century Asia. Besides Asia-focused content, a key example is the creation of residential colleges that integrate living and learning, with a level of investment in undergraduate facilities that is hard to imagine in the current North American, Western European or Australian public education context. This is partly because in Singapore (and elsewhere in Asia), undergraduates are considered an important "national" resource, and their cultivation is at least on par with research.[13]

To some extent this model also draws on the memory of what British Commonwealth colleges—including Raffles College, from which the National University of Singapore grew—were like in the early-to-mid twentieth century before they became research universities: melting pots where students and teachers from every department rubbed shoulders and exchanged ideas. But the Singaporean colleges are also the result of extensive study trips abroad to understand, contrast, and borrow from different college models around the globe, a characteristic Asian planning method that American institutions would do well to emulate.

COLLEGE COMMUNITIES IN THE LARGE RESEARCH-INTENSIVE UNIVERSITY

More than any word, "community" sums up the achievable aspirations of colleges, given their generally small sizes and their ethos of maximizing learning in and beyond the classroom. While UM Honors grew out of one of the oldest honors programs in the United States (established in 1935) it only became a college in 2003, and even more recently acquired dedicated dormitory space in order to offer a residential component. Tembusu, following the

Commonwealth model, stressed residency from its very beginning: students can only partake in the academic program if they live in the college, and *vice versa.*

While forming distinct communities, both colleges are integrally linked with the faculties and departments around them through the sharing of students and staff. While each has a small number of dedicated staff, many others are jointly appointed, or in some cases seconded from departments.[14] Neither college is thus an island unto itself; each is dependent in part on the goodwill of surrounding departments and institutes in order to thrive.

What attracts faculty to a position at the college is the prospect of furthering students' intellectual growth, in small classes and by exposing them to evocative, challenging materials and conversation across disciplines. An emphasis on experimentation in learning and teaching is part of both colleges' pedagogical ethos, as is support for students' individual development. Core faculty members working within the remit of interdisciplinarity in each of the colleges have to tread relatively unfamiliar ground in the respective universities,[15] but arrangements are in place to make this choice a viable alternative to the traditional tenure-in-the-discipline track.[16]

The pedagogical ethos underpins the colleges' efforts to find, and retain, curious, talented, and highly motivated students who want to be part of an interdisciplinary community. In recruiting students, both colleges emphasize that the learning environment they provide complements the advantages of being in a large research-intensive university, such as exposure to the latest research, access to extensive research infrastructure, and choice from a large range of majors.

UM Honors has attracted top students from the region who wanted an educational experience similar to that offered at private liberal arts colleges but without the hefty price tag. Like many other honors programs and the universities that house them, it espouses Frank Aydelotte's now-classic argument that the best undergraduates should be challenged and nurtured in a special program.[17] Echoing the perception of honors education as "ivy league education [within] state universities,"[18] Jamie Cox, then a first-year student at UM Honors, wrote that "short of schools costing thousands of dollars more than UMaine, the Honors Program affords [. . .] the very best in opportunities that students who work hard so richly deserve."[19]

Tembusu has attracted talented and motivated students intent on a more holistic university experience than their degree program alone would provide. As one of several colleges in the NUS landscape, and not the one perceived to be most "elite," it selects students not primarily on the basis of academic excellence but on motivation and perceived fit with the diverse living-learning environment it provides. Anecdotal evidence suggests that the existence of Tembusu and its sister colleges—as well as the more recently established Yale-NUS College—has helped the university attract some students who would otherwise have applied overseas.

In sum, in both Maine and Singapore, the two colleges offer many of their university's best and most motivated students the chance to take part in an interdisciplinary program that provides small-scale instruction and connection to peers and faculty members from multiple disciplines and backgrounds. Besides the commonalities discussed earlier, there are also significant differences in how each colleges puts its pedagogical ethos into practice and seeks to cultivate an attractive and generative atmosphere for students and staff alike.

In the next section, these differences are further explored. Such an exploration is part of the value of—and also informs—the building of meaningful bilateral ties, not least because some differences are representative of the educational, if not national, cultures in which the colleges are situated.

CONTRASTS IN THE TWO COLLEGE MODELS: AMERICAN HONORS VERSUS SINGAPOREAN GENERAL EDUCATION

The Core Curriculum

The core of the honors curriculum at Maine is a four-course Civilizations sequence, required for all first- and second-year honors students. The Civilizations sequence is a "Great Books" program that takes the students through some forty powerful texts, from the pre-Socratics to Coetzee via the Bible, Bacon, Marx, Nietzsche, etc. These texts are discussed in small groups facilitated by a preceptor, and they are contextualized and further explained in lectures by experts from across the university.

This emphasis on civilizations and their texts is recognized internationally as being a distinctly American curriculum. Indeed, it is similar in outline to the curriculum of Yale-NUS College in Singapore, a close neighbor of Tembusu, which offers one of the most authentically American liberal arts curricula in Asia.[20]

Tembusu does not have a "Great Books" curriculum. Rather than cultivating the individual through contact with the writing of great minds of present and past, courses are designed to foster interdisciplinary conversation by foregrounding topics, issues, and questions that are of broad interest or concern locally and/or globally, and that span the boundaries of several disciplines. Examples are "Social Innovation," "Living and Dying in the Internet Age," "Poetry and Science," "Fakes," "Disasters," and "Violence."

Many, though by no means all, Tembusu courses are oriented to the study of "Science, Technology, and Society." Courses such as the senior seminars on "Biomedicine and Singapore Society," "Technology and the Fate of Knowledge," and "Climate Change" help students critically to assess the ways of knowing and the technological arrangements we live by. They prompt students to engage with the assumptions, choices, pleasures, and responsibilities of science and technology inflected lives, and to develop an appreciation of different perspectives regarding these.

At Maine, all students and faculty members read the same corpus, and this helps create common intellectual ground. At the same time, it is understood that each preceptor's disciplinary background and pedagogical style will influence his or her approach and emphasis. Students are also explicitly encouraged to read these texts against and through their own experiences, developing and exchanging thoughts on what it means to be "human." Seminars are designed to cultivate habits of reading and relating that students take to their disciplinary courses, and that will benefit them throughout their lives.

At Tembusu, there are no courses which every student takes. The curriculum consists of five modules: two writing courses and three seminars, all taken in the first two years, with a choice of topics on offer every semester. The college balances student preferences with disciplinary diversity when allocating students to classes, which are capped at fifteen. Students are encouraged to find paths through these modules that are personally meaningful for them, and this is also what provides the basis for learning from one another.

Alongside essay or case-study writing assignments, seminars at Tembusu contain non-writing assignments such as the physical representation of climate relations in 3D maquettes or models, an intervention project to highlight aspects of the use of public space, and the development of a seminar-style lesson to be delivered to peers. When working on assignments for these courses, students are encouraged to experiment, that is, to go beyond what they know or can already do well. In line with this, they have the option to take all these courses on a pass/fail basis rather than receiving grades on their transcript.

All the above-mentioned features distinguish the Tembusu classroom from the typical educational experiences many of its students have had. Singapore's education system has long had a reputation for both being very good and very competitive. With this comes a pressure for the students to "do well" and for the teachers to differentiate students according to their level of performance. Although the tide is changing, this has traditionally made it challenging to encourage learners to take risks and collaborate, aspects that feature heavily in Tembusu's general education curriculum.

In Maine, "interdisciplinarity" means students and faculty will inhabit their own discipline but also engage with the texts of the Civilizations sequence, which cannot be "owned" by any one discipline but are conceived as heritage for all. By committing to giving these texts sustained attention, faculty members and students are forced to step away from expert identities and engage with each other in intelligent conversation without a special mandate for one way of seeing things over another.

The seminars at Tembusu are also designed to foster thinking across disciplines and beyond disciplinary boundaries. Many Tembusu faculty encourage students to contribute insights or examples from their own majors to the seminar discussion.[21] A life sciences student may expound on the biology of cancer during a discussion of the desirability of prostate cancer screening; a social work student may play a social worker in a multi-stakeholder debate about healthcare provisions for the elderly. By doing this, the multifaceted nature of an issue or topic comes to life, and students learn to make connections "out from" their major.

Faculty members at Tembusu have much freedom to design and teach seminar courses according to their own convictions. Indeed, the most unequivocal pedagogical principle underpinning Tembusu's academic program is that being in a small discussion-based class, with a diversity of voices, and a dedicated, motivated instructor *in and of itself benefits students*. In this environment, students continuously practice oral and written expression, are exposed to different points of view and given tailored feedback, and have the chance to co-determine the direction and pace of the course.

After the Core Curriculum

Tembusu's focus is on the first two years of its University's three or four-year degree programs. Students who complete its two-year general education program receive a certificate; due to space constraints only a minority can be accommodated for a third (and an even smaller group for a fourth) year in residence.

Students who are selected to stay often take on leadership and mentorship roles. In the third year, the college offers a series of workshops on cultivating self-awareness and "exploring possibilities." Students also initiate projects and engagements they feel stretch them appropriately and help them make the best use of the resources, networks, and infrastructure of the college. These have included, among others, starting a literary journal, reimagining student politics, setting up an urban garden, and becoming involved in a faculty member's teaching or research.

In the fourth year, when Tembusu can keep only fifteen to twenty students out of the original freshman intake of two hundred, students are offered one-on-one mentoring by a faculty or staff member of their choice. Such mentoring can connect with students' intellectual or professional interests, their hopes and concerns for life after graduation, and/or their activities in the college as mentors for others.

By contrast, at UM Honors the two-year liberal core is followed by an upper-level focus on a research or creative thesis. After the Civilizations sequence, students take an honors tutorial or equivalent of their choice, and an optional thesis preparation course before writing their honors thesis. The honors tutorials are eight-person seminar courses led by a faculty member who proposes the topic and organizes the class. This is a curricular space for faculty from throughout the University to contribute topically and pedagogically innovative classes to multidisciplinary groups of students.[22]

The thesis is a significant feature of the honors experience at UMaine, in that the college has built a reputation for supporting students in delivering rigorous and high-quality, often publishable work. Honors students at UMaine have significant leeway in defining their thesis topic and choosing their supervisors, to the extent that some of them settle on a project outside of their major and work mostly with honors faculty.

The Honors thesis process at the University of Maine culminates in a formal defense before a committee of five faculty members. The large committee and the 2.5-hour time slot allotted to the defense ensure that depth and rigor in the discipline, as well as breadth of intellectual and personal exploration, are probed in this final element of the honors experience. In addition, students prepare and discuss a personal annotated reading list composed of texts both from and beyond the Civilizations sequence. Completion of the thesis at UMaine adds an Honors certification to the four-year bachelor's degree.

Opportunities to Flourish

At Tembusu it is common for students to find fulfillment, expression, and self-discovery in pursuits that are not, or not directly, related to their academic studies. This is a result of its positioning in an environment where an experimental space of this kind—one in which students can try out different modes of expression and interaction with others—is not easily come by elsewhere.[23]

As an integrated living-and-learning environment, Tembusu's variegated spaces accommodate big and small-scale activities, events, and gatherings, both during the day and in the evening. From staging a musical production to running a high-performing debate team, from providing support for a school for street children in Cambodia to organizing daily Ultimate Frisbee trainings, from promoting the conservation of endangered species to the (self-)cultivation of a group of student-ambassadors hosting college guests, these outside-of-classroom activities profoundly shape the college experience.

Unlike Tembusu, where all students live in the same building and where enrollment in the academic program is conditional upon being a resident, honors students at Maine have different residential options on campus. There are a few dedicated honors buildings, where students bond and faculty and administration of the college are present in some of the same spaces frequented by students. Direct faculty influence on residential life is minimal, however, and the college is defined as first and foremost an intellectual and academic community.

Maine has made a more significant commitment than Tembusu to undergraduate research. A major hiring round in 2010–2011 emphasized the ideal of the "teacher-scholar," an academic who is a strong teacher and whose research accommodates, and is indeed in part designed to elicit, collaboration from undergraduate-researchers.[24] This role has helped to generate a research culture that is open, collaborative, and non-pretentious. Faculty members and students regularly attend conferences together, and publish jointly authored papers. Among other things, such activities allow students to test aptitude for and interest in pursuing graduate studies.

Recently the Honors College has started to create a series of *research collaboratives* to bring together students from a wide variety of majors with faculty from different disciplines and community partners to create so-called Knowledge-to-Action frameworks.[25] These collaborative arrangements embed students in community-engaged and interdisciplinary research.

The first of these, the Sustainable Food Systems Research Collaborative (SFSRC) brings together faculty from Honors, Public Policy, Business, Cooperative Extension/agriculture, and partners like the local food pantry, a local social justice group called *Food and Medicine*, and the University Dining Services.[26] A second collaborative, the Genomics Research Collaborative is being formed on the basis of an undergraduate training grant from the National Institutes of Health for Honors students in the biomedical sciences.[27]

In summary, despite their allegiance to discussion-based education, to interdisciplinarity and to personalized instruction, the two colleges differ in what is at the heart of their curriculum: "Great Books" for one, and a variety of interdisciplinary topics with a Science, Technology, and Society orientation for the other. They differ even more in what happens beyond the core curriculum: UM Honors is a stimulating environment for academic (often interdisciplinary and community-involved) research, whereas Tembusu supports a myriad of initiatives and engagements, many but not all with faculty involvement, to foster student development.

One way to characterize these differences is to say that the UM Honors' model for building learning communities begins from the academic side, whereas Tembusu's starts from the residential side. The interaction between the two colleges has spurred reflection on the way in which different models serve students raised in different educational and national cultures. It has also stimulated curiosity about the features of each college's approach that are most beneficial to students, and which of these features could be borrowed, adapted, or further developed through bilateral collaboration.

THE FUTURE: THOUGHTS, QUESTIONS, AND COLLABORATION

The global proliferation of colleges within universities that is currently underway provides a new opportunity for American honors programs to build bilateral connections that can enrich the lives and perspectives of individual faculty and students, but also of those programs as a whole. Embedded as they are within large, research-intensive universities, and committed to nurturing and challenging students beyond disciplinary boundaries, these programs provide an excellent basis for connecting to similar environments in different parts of the world.

In the case of the University of Maine Honors College and Tembusu College at the National University of Singapore, their identity as *learning communities* is at the center of their transnational college-to-college relationship. This is borne out by the informal, ad hoc approach to building links, the investment in discovering and discussing commonalities and differences, and the willingness to experiment with creating initiatives for mutual benefit.

The question of how geographical and cultural differences can be utilized in the engagement with global topics and concern, is now beginning to sprout plans and ideas. As students from Tembusu and UM Honors are asked together to reflect on complex, multifaceted problems, it is probable that the salient differences between the two contexts will help students make distinctions and reflect more deeply on what they take for granted in their own environment.

For example, a look at the climate change adaptation plans for Singapore and for the northeast United States brings out some similar concerns (sea level rise) but also some real differences: Singapore faces shortages of fresh water while Maine may face an increase in precipitation; Singapore grows 4 percent of its food while agriculture is an important sector of Maine's economy; Singapore's plan cites a focus on biodiversity and greenery while the plan for Maine notes that winter recreation (i.e., skiing) may become a thing of the past.[28]

Interdisciplinary engagement is not only important to the identity of the two colleges, but is also a project the colleges can come together to discuss, critique, and help each other more fully realize. Beyond interdisciplinarity, colleges can also learn from each other's ways to build a vibrant learning community, broadly conceived.

Two small examples include Tembusu's active consideration of adopting the UM "Honors Read" (a book sent to all entering students to read in the summer before they start at university); and UM Honors' formation of a

Board of Advocates to take on aspects of Tembusu's Rector, a role given to a nationally-known citizen whose job it is to help raise the college's profile outside the university.

Paradoxically, in an age of globalization, the "elite" status of colleges has been able to continue without much reference to global markers, a situation at once enviable (given pressures on departments and institutes) but ultimately limiting if it discourages global thinking and engagement. The college-to-college approach to building bilateral relations provides much scope for mutually beneficial dialogue and exchange regarding topical areas (global problems), pedagogies (interdisciplinarity) and strategies to support students' intellectual and personal growth in the college environment.

By providing learning opportunities associated with exposure to different geographical, cultural, and organizational contexts, such dialogue and exchange can provide new perspectives to students and faculty as well as invigorate the college as a learning community.

KEY IDEAS IN THIS CHAPTER

- The collegiate models that emerged out of British higher education share many objectives with honors education in the U.S., especially with the fully developed Honors College model articulated by NCHC.
- The recent establishment of colleges within universities in Asian countries and elsewhere provides opportunities for American honors programs and colleges to collaborate and internationalize, and for honors education to feature in universities' global branding efforts.
- Using the collegial foundation as a basis, cross-cultural collaboration between institutions operating in different national contexts can spur productive innovation in and reconsideration of strategic missions, student curricula, programmatic offerings, faculty models, and administrative functions.
- The experience of the Tembusu College at the National University of Singapore and the University of Maine Honors College discussed here offers one concrete example of the ways that partners can incrementally build meaningful relationships that enrich their respective institutions.

NOTES

1. Aaron M. Brower and Karen Kurotsuchi Inkelas, "Living-Learning: One High-Impact Educational Practice," *Liberal Education* 2 (Spring 2010): 36–43. For an earlier perspective, see S. Stewart Gordon, "Living and Learning in College," *The Journal of General Education* 25, no. 4 (1974): 235–245.

2. The Collegiate Way website run by Robert J. O'Hara lists colleges in the following countries: Australia, Canada, China, Germany, Ghana, Great Britain, India, Malaysia, Mexico, the Netherlands, New Zealand, Pakistan, Portugal, Singapore, Spain, and the United States. See http://collegiateway.org/colleges/, accessed March 11, 2016.

3. For example, UMaine's *College of Engineering* would be referred to as the *Faculty of Engineering* in Singapore.

4. Collegiate Way Conference 2014, University of Durham, accessed July 10, 2014, https://www.dur.ac.uk/collegiateway2014/.

5. National Collegiate Honors Council, *Official NCHC Online Guide to Honors Colleges and Programs*, May 2015, accessed June 25, 2015, http://nchchonors.org/news/nchc-online-guide-to-honors-programs-and-colleges, p. 353.

6. Tembusu College is one of four residential colleges on the University Town campus of the National University of Singapore. Tembusu College, the College of Alice and Peter Tan (CAPT) and Residential College 4 share a common curricular structure and organizational setup. The fourth college, Cinnamon, houses the sixteen-year old University Scholars Programme, which was partially based on Harvard's Core Curriculum Programme.

7. In 2014, 71 percent of UMaine Honors College students were in-state, a slightly lower percentage than for the undergraduate population as a whole (74 percent). In the academic year 2014/2015, 69 percent of Tembusu students were Singaporean citizens; if exchange students (who do not generally participate in the college's academic program but for whom Tembusu has an allotted number of rooms) are not counted, the percentage of local students was 79 percent.

8. An exception is certain college-like models which cater exclusively to international students, such as the "international houses" of the English-language "international colleges" sprouting up at Japanese universities.

9. Anthony Welch, "Higher Education in South-East Asia: Achievement and Aspiration," in *Education in South-East Asia (Oxford Series in Comparative Education)*, Ed. Colin Brock and Lorraine Pe Symaco, pp. 278–279 (Oxford: Symposium Books, 2011).

10. Kris Old, "Global Assemblage: Singapore, Foreign Universities, and the Construction of a 'Global Education Hub'," World Development 35, no. 6 (2007): 959–975.

11. Kenneth Paul Tan, "Service Learning Outside the U.S.: Initial Experiences in Singapore's Higher Education," *PS: Political Science & Politics* 42, no. 3 (2009): 555.

12. Tan Chorh Chuan, "Opportunities and Challenges Facing Asian Higher Education" (presentation at the 1st Asian University Presidents Forum, Guangzhou, China, November 12–14, 2010), accessed June 9, 2015, http://president.nus.edu.sg/pdf/forum.pdf.

13. Speech by Prime Minister Lee Hsien Loong at the Official Opening of University Town, National University of Singapore, October 17, 2013, accessed June 30, 2015, http://www.pmo.gov.sg/mediacentre/speech-prime-minister-lee-hsien-loong-official-opening-university-town.

14. For a deeper insight into the arrangements at the UM Honors College, see Robert W. Glover et al., "The Genesis of an Honors Faculty: Collective Reflections

on a Process of Change," *Honors in Practice* 8 (2012): 194. Tembusu has a close relationship to the Asia Research Institute, where almost half its staff have joint appointments.

15. Glover et al., "Genesis of an Honors Faculty."

16. In fall of 2013, six positions housed in whole or in part in the Honors College at UMaine were converted to tenure track and the holders of two of these positions have been awarded tenure. The National University of Singapore improved the job security and career progression opportunities of residential college faculty through the launch, in January 2015, of a new Educator Track that mirrors the tenure track in all but name.

17. Frank Aydelotte, *Breaking the Academic Lock Step: The Development of Honors Work in American Colleges and Universities* (New York: Harper and Row, 1944), cited in Norm Weiner, "Honors is Elitist, and What's Wrong with That?" *Journal of the National Collegiate Honors Council* 10, no. 1 (2009): 19–24.

18. Weiner, "Honors is Elitist," p. 21.

19. Jamie Cox, "Defending the Honors College," *The Maine Campus,* May 6, 2002.

20. Yale-NUS College Inaugural Curriculum Committee, Yale-NUS College: A New Community of Learning (Singapore: Yale-NUS College, 2013), accessed June 9, 2015, http://www.yale-nus.edu.sg/wp-content/uploads/2013/09/Yale-NUS-College-Curriculum-Report.pdf.

21. Although students are also given the freedom to leave their major "at the door" and try something different than inhabiting their budding disciplinary identity.

22. Recent and upcoming offerings include "Sustainable Food Systems: Principles, Practices, and Policies"; "Utopia, Dystopia, and Nature"; "Games as Culture and Vehicles of Change"; *Entartete Musik* (Degenerate Music); just to name a few. The tutorial alternative waives this requirement for students who study abroad or do an internship.

23. Michael M.J. Fischer, "Teaching under the Tembusu Tree: A Mandala for Education in the 21st Century, or The Self-Reengineering Mouse that Roars (Politely)," (unpublished manuscript, 2013).

24. Glover et al., "Genesis of an Honors Faculty," p. 194.

25. A Knowledge-to-Action framework, as advocated in fields such as sustainability science and climate change, is an arrangement in which scientific or knowledge communities work in liaison with communities of decision makers and other stakeholders. See, for example: David W. Cash et al., "Knowledge Systems for Sustainable Development," *Proceedings of the National Academy of Sciences* 100, no. 14 (2003): 8086–8091.

26. Two recent national presentations on this topic are: Mark Haggerty et al., "Promoting Honors Undergraduate Research: The Sustainable Food Systems Research Collaborative Model," (paper presented at the National Collegiate Honors Council Conference, Denver, CO, November 7, 2014); and François G. Amar et al., "Leveraging the Research Capacity of the Doctoral University for Honors Education: The 'Research Collaborative' Model," (paper presented at the second Biannual Conference on Honors Education at Research Universities, Corvallis, OR, May 19, 2015).

27. Maine INBRE supports research and training via an Institutional Development Award (IDeA) award from the National Institute of General Medical Sciences of the National Institutes of Health under grant number P20GM103423.

28. This passage draws on information from the website of the National Climate Change Secretariat (part of the Prime Minister's Office) in Singapore, on the "Impact of Climate Change on Singapore," accessed October 28, 2014, http://app.nccs.gov.sg/page.aspx?pageid=160& secid=157 and the website of the United States Environmental Protection Agency on "Climate Impacts in the Northeast," accessed July 15 2015, http://www.epa.gov/climatechange/impacts-adaptation/northeast.html.

Chapter 5

The Playful Curriculum

Differentiating Honors Education through the Use of Simulation as a Scaffold for Open-ended Course Design

Abby Loebenberg

A brief survey of contemporary research in the cognitive sciences reveals overwhelming support for the thesis that higher intelligence correlates strongly with streamlined neuron pathways and brain organization.[1] Further evidence shows that the role of the lateral prefrontal cortex (LPFC) is critical in controlling thought and behaviors, an activity known as executive function.

Executive function encompasses areas of brain function and development such as inhibition, shifting between ideas, and working memory. Moreover, the LPFC acts as a "global hub"[2] in controlling the neurological processes that are critical to intelligence. Children in particular show a strong correlation between the development of the LPFC[3] and typical development of executive function.

The timing in the life cycle of the development of this area of the brain and the shaping of neurological pathways coincides with an intensification of REM sleep and play, activities known to weed out poorly functioning pathways and promote the formation of new connections,[4] Children and young adults' behavior is anecdotally noted for its preference for both of these activities.

Play in particular, the focus of this chapter, is often said to be the core of curriculum for early childhood development: children learn through play. However, this is not free play of an undirected kind but rather play instrumentalized into a focused activity with a playful component, eliciting a response of fun or creativity. Examples of this in the early childhood classroom might be various types of physical or spatial coordination activities, such as gymnastics or block play.[5]

However, almost no emphasis is placed on the pedagogical value of play in higher education. This is despite the fact that play and sleep's associated neurological benefits in shaping and refining neurological pathways continue to be critical throughout the life span. Play, in addition to being pleasurable, is characterized (across species) as evolutionarily adaptive, testing limits in non-life-threatening situations.[6] In this sense, play is evolutionarily adaptive for the purposes of responding to the unfamiliar, essentially mapping new neurological connections.

Play is part of the neurological work of our lifetimes and is essential to the area of the brain known to be the hub of all intelligence processes (LPFC). Play is a preferred behavior for children and young adults, and, honors education, insofar as we accept that intelligence is a primary selection factor for students in these programs, should make its primary goal experimentation with new pedagogies that allow students to creatively, that is playfully, explore concepts rather than content.

One of the most well-recognized models in studies of creativity in psychology, the "Four-C" model of creativity, supports this position. The smallest creative act is called "mini-c" creativity, defined as "novel and personally meaningful interpretation of experiences, actions and events."[7] This is the type of creative and transformative moment inherent in the learning process and is the building block for other types of personal creative acts.

However, it is important to have a term for this "building block" type of creativity as previous creativity studies have only considered creativity in terms of the levels of "creative genius" necessary for professional creative success or super-success.[8] How does one compare enjoying painting on the weekends (termed little-c in this model) to being a professional portrait artist (Pro-c), to being a recognized genius, such as Leonardo da Vinci (Big-C)?

Is it definitionally adequate simply to talk of students as being "creative" or of educators "creating" courses without having benchmarks for the types of creativity they might be employing to do so? Thus, discussing and defining creativity and its developmental corollary playfulness adequately serves two purposes.

On a broader level, it is the author's argument that the honors college of the future should be a place of creativity and rupture where the faculty and administrators themselves are, committed to goals of pedagogical innovation and experimentation, that they should hold themselves to the standard of being professionally creative (Pro-c) in this area. James C. Beghetto and Ronald A. Kaufmann indicate that developing Pro-c expertise usually requires formal training, publication and ongoing innovation in an area over a period of, on average, ten years.

This is not significant news to those in academia, whose academic careers mark this trajectory closely. However, this chapter suggests that educators pay closer attention to the idea that honors education itself is a discipline, not a secondary interest, and that those who pursue it fully have become interdisciplinarians by its very nature. This breaking down of boundaries happens as soon as the honors college classroom door opens and is an opportunity educators should shape very deliberately.

This chapter documents research into using an experimental and open-ended play-based, creative pedagogy for honors classes. The first is a simulation created from an existing anthropological case study in order to demonstrate the efficacy of games to communicate complex concepts, and the other a course design based on an existing paper role-playing game platform with reference to a well-tested course structure known as *Reacting to the Past*.

These new class models offer challenges to the timing and class structure traditionally used in the U.S. semester system, and offers the suggestion that playful curriculum design speaking to the biological and developmental strengths of young adults is an area of potential differentiation in honors education. This will point to future directions for design of a playful and open-ended curriculum wherein honors educators can innovate as pedagogical leaders with courses structured around the building blocks of creativity and led by professionals who see themselves as primarily engaged in honors education as a discipline in its own right.

PLAY AND CREATIVITY

The National Collegiate Honors Council (NCHC) makes only one passing reference to the idea of creativity in its definition of honors and honors education and no reference to play. NCHC notes that honors education "help(s) students understand how scholars think about problems, formulate hypotheses, research those problems, and draw conclusions about them; and to help students understand how creative artists approach the creative process and produce an original work."[9]

This understanding of "how scholars and artists work" is defined as the fourth objective of honors education as listed on the organization's website, and seems awkward in a number of ways, particularly as it seems assumptive that creative and scholarly processes parallel each other implicitly. It is probably desirable that scholarly processes are creative, in the sense that their products are in some way innovative, but the emphasis on process may be misleading.

The creative process is often seen as instinctive or in some senses a "black box,"[10] that is to say that concept and material are transformed in the mind of the artist and emerge as the creative product. Even where "process" is visible, the precise mechanism of this transformation is unclear; it is attributed to the inspiration of the Muse, named for the Greek word *mosthai*, which translates as, "making philosophical enquiries."[11]

The other understanding of the creative process views it as inexplicable or a type of mysterious or subconscious genius. A number of authors have recently explored the sociology of creative collectives and groups and have argued that the role of friendship and collaboration is far more significant in the role of the creation of "genius" level creativity than is commonly recognized.[12]

Moreover, these studies of genius creativity tend not to discuss much the journeyman creative, the person who makes their living as a "Pro-c" creative using the Kaufmann and Beghetto language. These individuals have far more in common with undergraduates learning their individual disciplines than undergraduates have in common with genius-level creatives in their fields.

Similarly, the scholarly process is often written of, and taught, as an invocation of the knowledge canon of a particular field. While creativity or inspiration may strike in order to bring ideas or concepts together, this alone is not sufficient; the scholar must support ideas, and trace a logical path through thesis and argument. To simply point to a "black box" of so-called genius and shrug one's metaphorical shoulders is not sufficient.

In this sense the scholarly process more closely resembles the Japanese system of *Meisho-Deshi* (literally master-apprentice) where the apprentice learns the *kata* (form) of their discipline through mimesis and progresses through ranks of achievement as they strive for the ideal form that previous masters have demonstrated. Only once an individual is recognized as a master in their own right is innovation in any form permitted or validated.[13]

This process is what one might see as genius-level creativity expressed in the sciences or technology where access to facilities and resources are controlled by gatekeepers generally supported by apprenticeships through the academy. However, especially in the case of the technology or scientific greats, for example Albert Einstein, their relationship with the academy is often underplayed in favor of a (often mythical) "self-taught maverick" theory.[14]

Seemingly, the Western notion of artistic creativity is often conceived of as the individual operating in some sort of "genius bubble," an entirely fictive notion when examined in historical or sociological context.[15] In the definition of cultural anthropologists the "creative persona" is one that produces a "transformation of existing cultural practices"[16] and as such produces as "eruption"[17] in the social order.

In this sense, social structure is seen as the conscious and ongoing set of cultural practices of a group of individuals who produce and sustain it. This structure forms the frame of reference for mediating and shaping individual experience, however it does not entirely capture or determine that experience holistically. Acting creatively, in this sense, is to act as a true individual, perhaps, in a sense to be the model, or even, "role-model" individual that the genius-level creative represents.

However, the "eruptions" to the social order that creativity brings, as they gain traction and social acceptance (and divorce themselves from their creator), become mired in the context from which they emerge. These new forms become the old, institutionalized ones, becoming ordinary, even though the drive to creativity and individuality is not lost. While looking toward great acts of creative genius for inspiration is helpful, the prevalence of Big-C creative genius in society is comparatively rare. The NCHC definition seems to refer only to this limited, Big-C version of creativity, confining the study of creativity to one of retrospection, not innovation.

This narrowness is unfortunate, as it has been found in the limited amount of research done with college students that they perceive the majority of their creative contributions as connected with everyday interactions and experiences, that is, mini-c and little-c creativity.[18] If the NCHC's limited definition of their sphere of learning seems disappointing, it is incumbent on honors courses to create space for creativity as "eruption," rather than codifying creative acts and absorbing them into the canonical quagmire.

Inherently, such a course design would be open-ended and each iteration deliberately unique. The reality of such a course seems inherently impractical in an administrative sense. How is an open-ended course assessed? How is it taught, and does it fit into a semester schedule? How are the credit hours assigned and evaluated? How is it accounted for in terms of extra preparation time for faculty members? This institutional quicksand is inherently at odds with creation. However, there is an ephemeral quality to the creative eruption that indicates its inherent flexibility to be invoked in the course of conventional pedagogy.

PEDAGOGICAL QUESTIONS, PLAYFUL SOLUTIONS

In order to offer some solutions for these pedagogical questions one might begin with Lev S. Vygotskian's theory, which is increasingly canonical in education departments globally.[19] This literature has offered the term "scaffold"[20] as a descriptor for pedagogical activities that allow students to build a framework allowing for a larger task to be accomplished.

This derives from Vygotsky's original notion of the "Zone of Proximal Development"[21] (ZPD), which describes an area of achievement between what a learner can and cannot do, often seen to be the area of understanding that learners can be guided to by a facilitator. Thus, in the sense of the creative, eruptive act, the scaffold might be some type of structure, assignment, activity, or facilitation method that primes the students to produce those acts.

To return momentarily to the neurological basis underpinning this thinking, consider the difference between the neurological pathways in the brains of artists and nonartists and whether there is a way to emulate or form those types of connections for honors students in training. Dahlia Zaidel, reviewing the literature on the effects of brain damage in specific regions of the brain to artists, concludes that the production of art is a "multi-process activity"[22] and that no one area of the brain or set of pathways is responsible.

Furthermore, multiple redundancies are built into the brain so that even in cases where one hemisphere of the brain is severely damaged or dementing diseases are present, artistic production continues to take place until there is widespread neuronal connectivity loss (particularly at the end of diseases). Thus, one might extrapolate that activities that encourage the brain to produce multiple neural pathways and to make connections that "prepare for the unexpected"[23] that is to say, playful activities, are an important facilitator for creative acts.

This conclusion is widely supported across disciplinary fields.[24] In a qualitative sense while play does not necessarily lead to creative expertise in a specific area of the arts, play can be a foundation for the type of open-mindedness and exploration of possibilities imaginatively that leads to creativity. In other words, play is an important part of the ZPD for creativity.

Without a doubt, when play is instrumentalized and harnessed into the classroom it takes on a different form than it does when it arises spontaneously. Moreover, young adults (and adults) are not likely to perceive their activities as characteristically playful. However, young adults do indisputably play.

Mark C. Carnes, creator of the *Reacting to the Past* series of role-immersion games, labels this play as "subversive"[25] yet also names students' interest in competitive gaming as the inspiration for his reimagination of the history classroom. *Reacting* games modify the role-playing game format into a more rigid framework where students have the freedom to explore interactions among their roles, but are constrained to preset roles, scenarios, and modes of engagements (e.g., speech making and essay writing), that are assessable and meet requirements for general studies contexts.

Reacting began at Barnard College in the 1990s and is now taught in many classrooms for its engaging qualities in place of United States History I and II and World Civilization. It demonstrates that a scaffold for playful activities is likely to make the most sense in the educational context. The argument that games as a form of scaffolding are effective in the college classroom is also made by Janna Jackson based on her use of videogame-like components to motivate student participation and success.[26]

Jackson's argument is that the strategies used by videogames to engage players can be used similarly in technology and non-technology-based classes to engage students because there is a parallel between the idea of the ZPD and the ways in which videogames are successful at adapting to the competence of the user and providing them just enough challenge to keep them interested.

Jackson argues that *Reacting to the Past* also targets the ZPD through the role-playing approach. However, her article and Mark C. Carnes' self-reflections are seemingly the only literature that engages with long-term use of role-playing games in the college classroom. Her argument that attributes of video games could make college courses more successful differentiates her work from that on video-game use in education, and thus marks it as an under-documented area.

What both video and role-playing games have in common as learning scaffolds are what psychologist Mikail Csikzentmihalyi calls "flow,"[27] that is the loss of a sense of time that comes through total absorption in an activity. This is also reported by Carnes' students in his *Reacting* courses. Data collected about game players demonstrates "an increased appetite for risk, a greater comfort with failure, a stronger desire for social affiliations, a preference for challenges, a capacity for independent problem-solving, and a desire to be involved in meaningful work when compared with nongamers."[28]

This type of behavior might be argued to be particularly desirable as a counterbalance to the risk-averse, grade-obsessed student that seems to represent the typical applicant to honors colleges.[29] Caveats to the unfairness of the previous statement aside, the root of these behaviors seems to be tied to the educational approaches utilized and accolades awarded at the high-school level.

HONORS VERSUS GIFTED AND TALENTED EDUCATION

The emergence of "honors student" as a label can, arguably, be traced to similar roots as the creation of special programming for gifted and talented middle and high-school students. It is particularly revealing to consider how these students are defined, what types of educational philosophies are applied toward their success and how they are programmed for.

The literature on gifted and talented programs is interesting, as there is nothing that immediately suggests a connection with the creative open-ended game-based classroom. However, what is present in the literature is revealing. The United States Education department first defined gifted and talented in the Elementary and Secondary Education Act of 1969 as follows:

> Gifted and talented children are those identified by professionally qualified persons who by virtue of outstanding abilities, are capable of high performance.

These are children who require differentiated educational programs and/or services beyond those normally provided by the regular school program in order to realize their contribution to self and society. Children capable of high performance include those with demonstrated achievement and/or potential ability in any of the following areas, singly or in combination:

1. generally intellectual ability
2. specific academic aptitude
3. *creative* or productive thinking [emphasis added]
4. leadership ability
5. visual or performing arts
6. psychomotor ability

It can be assumed that utilization of these criteria for identification of the gifted and talented will encompass a minimum of 3 to 5 percent of the school population.[30]

This definition has been updated, but substantially remains the same. The strategies the Act identifies as suitable for a differentiated education program to meet these learners' needs are in line with those of Vygotskian practice, including special groupings like honor classes, a differentiated curriculum and instructional strategies that accommodate the learning styles of the gifted and talented.

The reality of these programs is that they have, over their history, been funded and unfunded multiple times and expensive items (like special classes) are rare, and also understudied. John F. Feldhusen's synthesis of research on gifted students does discuss special groupings, but explains that the main focus of the literature surrounds their social value, research on bullying and so on, rather than their academic nature.[31]

Moreover, special groupings tend to be interest classes such as robotics, technology or astronomy with developmental rather than academic value. That is to say that novel pedagogical strategies here do not necessarily cross-pollinate to the bulk of classes. The core focus of the gifted program is acceleration; "do more, do it faster" seems to be the order of the day. The solution for students' boredom in class is to send them more briskly through the curriculum ahead of their peers.

Concerns raised about the emotional development of students accelerated beyond their grade level were addressed by an oft-cited, 1984 study by James A. Kulik and Chen-Lin Kulik that is still a benchmark in this area.[32] Emphasis in gifted programs is placed on taking the Scholastic Aptitude Test (SAT) test early, as is on the Advanced Placement (AP) examinations. Feldhusen states:

Several researchers have reported on studies in which middle school and high school students received advanced high school or college level courses while still enrolled as secondary students. . . . Compared to students of equal ability who did not take AP courses, students who did so in high school had better academic records in college, graduated from college with more honors, engaged in more leadership activities, and took more advanced courses in college.[33]

Feldhusen's ringing support for acceleration as the ultimate cornerstone of gifted and talented education seems to assume that his reported findings remain valid when extrapolated indefinitely, suggesting that simply taking more and more AP classes will ensure college success. This is of course ridiculous, which should be kept in mind when choosing student to admit into the honors college of the future.

However, what of the middle and early high-school years? Since the 1970s, differentiated teaching and modifications for individual learning style have stood as the federal guidelines for a good gifted education. However, the reality is, as Sally Reis et al. discovered, that 84 percent of gifted students received no differentiation in the classroom whatsoever,[34] and those that do receive only minor modifications to assignments.[35] This is despite a survey finding that 90 percent of high-school teachers think that differentiation is important in the classroom.[36]

The idea of classroom differentiation and the ZPD remain an important part of gifted education in principle, but this need arguably cannot be met by the de facto current practice, simply taking more and more AP classes.[37] This may, however, explain a little of the typical honors students' character. Game-based assignments and courses have the ability to truly challenge creativity and engage with flow in a way that is open-ended and compatible with neuro-positive playful behavior.

Building on these principles, and applying the author's own disciplinary reflexivity, the following two examples of facilitations from the author's teaching practice in honors anthropology will be presented in order to analyze the structure that underpins their pedagogical value. The case studies follow two patterns, one an actual cultural example that is reimagined as a game, the second a game recorded socially.

The first is derived from an actual cultural example that is designed to present the complexity of social and symbolic exchange in a nonmonetary economy and allow students to reflect on these challenges through simulation. The second uses an existing open-ended role-playing game framework in order to create an in-classroom opportunity to document and write an ethnography[38] of a set of complex social interactions. The first example takes approximately an hour to play; the second is the blueprint for a one-credit-hour semester-long course.

TEACHING THE *KULA*-RING SYMBOLIC EXCHANGE SYSTEM

The *kula* ring is a classic cultural anthropological case study featured in most textbooks and introductory courses to the subject. It is an example of a highly complex nonmonetary exchange system that originates in the Trobriand Islands (Melanesia). The total system of exchange in the Trobriands has multiple levels of transaction from produce (*wasi*) to manufactured goods (*gimwali*) to the symbolic and ceremonial exchange of *kula* goods themselves, which take the form of necklaces and armbands made from shells.

Some *kula* have names and genealogies attached to them. The purpose of *kula* is to circulate them; they have no value if hoarded, but the relative prestige of the *kula* that are gifted in these symbolic exchanges, and with whom the exchanges are made, is part of a system of alliances that facilitate successful transactions in other forms of exchange, such as *gimwali* exchange of canoes, pots, adzes, and so on.[39] In the *kula* ring armshells and necklaces are traded by a delegation from each island in different directions around the archipelago, either clockwise or counterclockwise, and multiple islands may be visited in a trip.[40]

The challenge for Western students is to understand the social motivations behind this system, which they initially perceive as incredibly strange and unnecessarily complex. Students also struggle to perceive the necessity for trade with neighboring islands for enriching quality of life on an island by obtaining goods that are specialized tools or merely decorative items.

The goal behind the simulation is to help them experience a condensed version of the system in order to help them internalize the social motivations behind how such a system develops. The development of cultural sensitivity toward Trobrianders' motivations is one of the most remarked-upon reflections that participants have been surprised to develop through playing this simulation.

Another important variable in student's perceptions of the simulation is whether the winning condition is revealed prior to the start of play or only at the end of play. Players who are told that the object of the simulation is to achieve as balanced a portfolio of resources as possible by the end of the game, but who are not explicitly told the distribution of resources (only their relative importance), give positive feedback more directed at understanding the isolation challenges of island life than other groups who are told the resource distribution in advance.

These groups also spend more time on strategy and change their strategies between rounds. Variations on strategies can be subtle such as deciding to let others see their trade goods versus hiding them; groups might be overly generous in one round hoping for reciprocity later or groups may try to leverage their positive *kula* relations for better trade in subsequent rounds.

When groups are told the resource distribution ahead of time (and the winning condition), the island that starts with the majority of the most valuable but scarcest resource immediately becomes a target, and they realize the power that they have over the other islands. In this scenario the players often express frustrations when islands refuse to trade with them or demand exorbitant prices for their goods.

Emphasizing positive *kula* relationship becomes more important as the scoring of the *kula* objects themselves can make a difference in the final outcome. In a sense this parallels the reality of the situation more closely, but makes the simulation less thought-provoking and seemingly less fun, illustrating the careful balance that must sometimes be found between real-world accuracy and pedagogical effectiveness.

OBSERVATIONS IN HONORS TEACHING

The *kula*-ring simulation is designed to be played in about one hour and is therefore appropriate for a single class period. The nature of exchange systems, being inherently transactional, renders them uniquely suited to adaptation into a game-like simulation. One of the key qualities of play is, as Gadamer puts it, a to-and-fro motion,[41] and this is core to the compatibility between exchange and games such as this example, or even game-theory games, such as the Prisoner's Dilemma,[42] which can also be physically simulated.

The advantage of simulation, as is clear through its use in aviation training for example, is that it requires students to inhabit a fixed perspective, in this case that of Trobrianders, in order to be successful. Particularly for honors students, who have often been through gifted and talented programs that emphasize acceleration, the "drive to win" is one that is highly motivating and pushes them into adopting a way of thinking that can override their ethnocentric ideas about the superiority of market exchange.

This process happens subconsciously throughout the game and a metacognitive exercise at the conclusion, asking them to reflect upon their decision-making processes, is critical to concretizing the learning value embodied in the simulation. As such, the simulation itself is clearly the scaffold to the (not so) simple task of putting oneself in another's shoes, that is, to achieve the emic perspective sought after in sociocultural anthropology.

Jackson's work on the adoption of videogame motivators in her college classroom suggests that this drive to win might be strong for many students. One of the techniques she uses is "leveling,"[43] where students have to achieve a certain amount of points before their next assignment would be available.

They could also complete each assignment at one of three levels, "Proficient," "Expert," or "Guru,"[44] with an increasing number of points attached to each level.[45]

This type of assignment construction demonstrates the use of differentiation, a ZPD and a "win" motivation in a classroom environment. Although it seems to apply more readily to a closed-skilled type of course, is a useful tool for building more complex assignments and open-ended coursework.

GURPS (GENERIC UNIVERSAL ROLE-PLAY SYSTEM) AND TEACHING ETHNOGRAPHIC METHODS

Writing ethnography, which forms the core of "doing" anthropology (among other social sciences), is complex to teach well, but simple to do. In fact, it is at the heart of the City as Text® methods that are used as part of the experiential learning courses taught by Bernice Braid[46] as a core part of NCHC conferences for many years. These are essentially an adaptation of a micro-ethnographic exploration, without its productive, that is, written, component, or the extended time-frame that characterizes ethnography.

Students, who are frequently unaware of the need for cultural sensitivity and awareness of other cultural viewpoints, often seek ways to engage with and write about culture. The value of immersion and ethnographic research, adopting an active rather than passive role in cultural practices and taking months or years to get to know another culture well, is immediately apparent to such students.

However, the primary hurdle for teaching ethnography is not one of pedagogy, but of bureaucracy; despite its low impact on those being observed, and the emphasis placed on informed consent, ethnographic research still generally requires Institutional Review Board (IRB) approval. This is not without its reasons, and those reasons should not be lightly discounted. Student security will also always be a concern in these scenarios, as ethnography is characteristically a solo activity.

While going through the lengthy IRB approval process may be a valid piece of research methods training, it is not compatible with a playful or creative experience, and it certainly teaches nothing about doing ethnography itself. The difficulty of finding a "field" for undergraduates to go into means that truly doing ethnography is often left for graduate school.

Even in the graduate context the field is arcane and students are unhelpfully told that they will "know what to do once they are there." Fieldwork has become a rite of passage for the anthropologist and an induction into a club of post-fieldwork initiates, after which one presumably understands the struggle of a year (or more) of fieldwork.

While this induction into the "anthropology club" is all well and good for the purposes of disciplinary solidarity, mystifying the experience of doing ethnography in the field does nothing to give students an understanding of what an effective qualitative tool it is, or how they might approach its challenges. The result is that virtually no students do ethnographic research for undergraduate honors theses, and those who attempt it do it poorly due to lack of experience.

Thus, qualitative theses become litanies of dull interviews with no context or true understanding of the life-worlds of those being studied, and seem inherently juvenile and weak. More and more honors colleges include nods to multiculturalism on syllabi and in mission statements. In this context, presenting sequences of classes that creatively engage with methods training in ways suitable for producing critical undergraduate-researchers may produce concrete steps toward these goals, but also interesting interdisciplinary projects that dialogue between students' major fields of studies and other fields such as anthropology or sociology.

However, students are unlikely to engage with a methods training class outside of their discipline if it is presented in a boring, linear way. Equally, the challenge for methods classes is to find a way to apply their training for students without violating IRB, or indeed ethics rules in general. An experimental solution to this problem of ethnographic research is to build on the success of *Reacting to the Past* and use a complex, socially interactive role-playing game platform (such as *GURPS*) as a scaffold to create the types of complex interactions that a student would face in an ethnographic setting.

That such a process will be fun and creative is guaranteed due to the success of the *GURPS* system itself as a leisure activity worldwide. Furthermore, the success of *Reacting* games, despite many of them omitting the random chance that is integral to role-playing games (usually dice throws), inspires confidence in the slightly bizarre world of *GURPS* to simulate the vagaries of real life for the ethnographic trainee.

The process of learning to do ethnography encompasses primarily participant observation in a social setting, making headnotes, and then, later, field notes about time spent in that setting and then, often some time later, writing the notes up into longer field memos which form the basis from which ethnographic comparisons can be made.[47] These note making and writing skills can all be practiced in a creative and playful context.

The strangeness (and perhaps awkwardness) of a *GURPS* world is no different to the reality of being an ethnographer in a new and unfamiliar cultural context. The goal of the class is both to provide training to the student, and also that the ethnographies resulting from this process will fuse the creative, playful, and academic in a way that is unique to that particular set of interactions and characters (and would differ from class to class).

ENVISIONING THE *GURPS* TABLE AS FIELD SITE

Three complete beginners to *GURPS* sit around a low table with a Game Master (GM) who is an experienced role-playing game player looking at them expectantly. The table is covered in notebooks, character sheets (ways to track and calculate the attributes of each character) and manuals for the game. The three players are trial-running a simplified version of *GURPS* with a preset story-scenario called "Caravan to Ein Arris"[48] that is designed to be open-ended. One player is laughing hysterically, her character meeting an unfortunate scenario that she is clumsily reacting to.

Deadpan, the GM asks, "What do you do?" The player responds and a dice roll is made. Again, it is not in her favor. A second character intervenes, role-playing the part of a prospective colleague. Moving between in-game speak and out-of-game speak is a challenge this early on and the character ends up "offending" her potential rescuer who abandons her to her fate. Things look bleak and the GM ends the day, telling her to "get lost" in his current role as a caravan-guard recruiter (a non-player character voiced by the GM) and then, switching to out-of-game speak advises the character to try her luck tomorrow with another recruiter.

The atmosphere of the game is incredibly absorbing even using preset scenario material and with the clumsy interactions of highly embarrassed new players. *GURPS* can be intimidating to begin and, as a generic role-play platform, overwhelming in the number of skills, attributes, and personality quirks it is possible to build into a character. However, there are simplified systems (*GURPS Lite*) and pre-created characters available that can allow beginners to get a feel for the experience in under an hour. A sense of collaborative story telling characterizes the *GURPS* scenario, as does a thrilling sense that anything could happen (in the game).

It is both the mechanical potential of the *GURPS* scenario to provide fodder to teach ethnography and its narrative content that marks its potential out as a scaffold for creativity. Creating narrative and particularly, framing our experiences in terms of narrative resonates strongly with how humans make and form social connections. Narratives are both a way to create order in time and to replace existing orders with new ones.[49]

Narratives inherently encapsulate both what is commonly understood and the possibilities that were passed over in creating that narrative. As such, their creative process is embedded within their product and those products are commonly differentiated, "fiction" versus "nonfiction" etc. Through *GURPS* however, that process of meaning-making is made visible; it is both fantasy and reality.

As is eloquently put by Anthony P. Kerby, "Narratives are a primary embodiment of our understanding of the world, of experience, and ultimately of ourselves. . . . It is in and through various forms of narrative emplotment that our lives—our very selves—attain meaning."[50] In that sense, as a form of meaning-making, *GURPS* ties in to one of humankind's most fundamental traditions, storytelling. However, it is also encoded with the type of game motivation that Jackson found motivated her students to keep going in her courses, such as leveling up and so on.

In the case of *GURPS*, it is the character that levels up and not the student, a critical difference particularly when it comes to risk-taking. Does one take more risks with one's character, does one's persona change, how is one's voice different and how do students reflect on that difference? These questions will only be answered through future research, however, previous studies certainly indicate that the potential for success is there.

CONCLUSION

Open-ended class structures offer opportunities to better engage with "how scholars and artists work"[51] not by seeing scholarly and creative processes as distinct, but by participating in the construction and criticism of these processes directly. Models that break down the types of creativity, such as the "Four-C" model, are invaluable here as they offer an opportunity to re-envision what types of creative contributions that students and honors professionals can make and how those contribute to teaching and learning practices.

Through acknowledging these contributions and encouraging creative pedagogical strategies and models the honors college of the future can emerge as a site of leadership to meet the needs of gifted and talented students and also to address some of the deficits that occur through the over-emphasis on acceleration and the practical lack of differentiation in the high-school gifted and talented context.

Moreover, immersion and simulation games in the classroom, as an example of this reform, are well-supported in terms of the literature on the effect of play on the cognitive development of adolescents. The examples given should also underscore the pedagogical value of engaging students in this way. It is no surprise to those working with college students that they seem more and more disengaged by the humanities, seeing their "Great Books" honors classes as a chore and the thesis as a roadblock rather than an opportunity.

The tearing forces of pre-professionalism and the opportunities for subversive play presented by social life at college (perhaps denied to honors students in previous education) seem an insurmountable obstacle for those trying to ignite a passion for knowledge for its own sake. If the honors classroom cannot do this in the contemporary educational context, is there hope for the general studies classroom? The opportunity for creative eruption (and perhaps disruption) and the creation of new learning forms lies with honors faculty, and we should embrace the risk of experimentation as we work to define and establish the honors colleges of tomorrow.

KEY IDEAS IN THIS CHAPTER

- Though "play" is a central feature of early childhood education, it is significantly less prevalent in later stages of education, despite substantial empirical research suggesting it remains an important component of human cognitive, social, and educational development.
- Honors education presents unique pedagogical opportunities for thinking about the possibilities of play as a component of teaching and learning, but will require innovation and flexibility on the part of honors faculty and their programs/colleges.
- Specific examples such as role play as a teaching tool in cultural anthropology or utilizing simulations as a means to learn the skills necessary for ethnographic research suggest the ways that we could think about incorporating play into honors education.

NOTES

1. See Earl K. Miller and Jonathan D. Cohen, "An Integrative Theory of Prefrontal Cortex Function," *Annual Review of Neuroscience* 24, no. 1 (2001): 167–202; Michael Cole et al., "Global Connectivity of Prefrontal Cortex Predicts Cognitive Control and Intelligence," *The Journal of Neuroscience* 32, no. 26 (2012): 8988–8999.

2. Cole et al., "Global Connectivity," p. 8988.

3. Yusuke Moriguchi and Kazuo Hirake, "Prefrontal Cortex and Executive Function in Young Children: a Review of NIRS Studies," *Frontiers in Human Neuroscience* 7 (2013): 1–9.

4. Stuart Brown and Christopher Vaughan, *Play: How it Shapes the Brain, Opens the Imagination and Invigorates the Soul* (New York: Avery/Penguin, 2009).

5. Lynn Cohen and John Uhry, "Young Children's Discourse Strategies During Black Play: A Bakhtinian Approach," *Journal of Research in Childhood Education* 21, no. 3 (2007): 302–315.

6. Marek Spinka, Ruth Newberry, and Marc Bekoff, "Mammalian play: Training for the Unexpected," *Quarterly Review of Biology* 76 (2001): 141–168.

7. James C. Beghetto and Ronald A. Kauffman, "Beyond Big and Little: The Four C Model of Creativity," *Review of General Psychology* 13, no. 1 (2009): 3.

8. See Keith Sawyer, *Explaining Creativity: The Science of Human Innovation* (Oxford: Oxford University Press, 2006); Randall Collins, *The Sociology of Philosophies: A Global Theory of Intellectual Change* (Harvard, MA: Belknap Harvard University Press, 2002).

9. National Collegiate Honors Council, "Definition of Honors Education," accessed July 1, 2015, http://nchchonors.org/wp-content/uploads/2014/02/Definition-of-Honors-Education.pdf; National Collegiate Honors Council, "Honors Course Design," accessed July 1, 2015, http://nchchonors.org/faculty-directors/ honors-course-design/.

10. Black box is a computing term that refers to an abstraction where components externally visible results are all that are considered, not the internal workings.

11. Plato. *Cratylus*. 2006, accessed June 14, 2014, http://www.ellopos.net/elpenor/greek-texts/ancient-greece/plato/plato-cratylus.asp?pg=28.

12. Such as Sawyer 2006, *Explaining Creativity*; Collins 2002, *The Sociology of Philosophies*; and John N. Parker and Edward J. Hackett, "Hot Spots and Hot Moments in Scientific Collaborations and Social Movements," *American Sociological Review* 77, no. 21 (2012): 21–44.

13. Brian Moeran, *Folk Art Potters of Japan: Beyond an Anthropology of Aesthetics* (Honolulu: University of Hawaii Press, 1998); Boye De Mente, *Elements of Japanese Design,* North Clarendon, VT: Tuttle Publishing, 2011.

14. Jesus Diaz, "Einstein Actually Had Excellent Grades," accessed May 30, 2015, http://gizmodo.com/5884050/einstein-actually-had-excellent-grades.

15. Sawyer, *Explaining Creativity,* 2002.

16. Smader Lavie, Kirin Narayan, and Renato Rosaldo, *Creativity/Anthropology* (Ithaca: Cornell University Press, 1993), pp. 5–6.

17. Ladislav Holy and Milan Stuchlik, "The Structure of Folk Models," in *The Structure of Folk Models*, Ed. Ladislav Holy and Milan Stuchlik (London: Academic Press, 1981), pp. 15–16.

18. Mark A. Pachucki, Jennifer C. Lena, and Steven J Tepper, "Creativity Narratives Among College Students: Sociability and Everyday Creativity," *The Sociological Quarterly* 51 (2010): 122–149.

19. Lev S. Vygotsky, *The Vygotsky Reader*, Ed. Rene Van der Veer and Jaan Valsiner (Oxford: Wiley-Blackwell, 1994).

20. Dorothy Faulkner, Karen Littleton, and Martin Woodhead, *Learning Relationships in the Classroom* (London and New York: Routledge, 2013).

21. Lev S. Vygotsky, *Mind in Society*, Ed. Michael Cole, Vera John-Steiner, Sylvia Scribner, and Elen Souberman (Cambridge: Harvard University Press, 1978); Lev S. Vygotsky, *The Collected Works of L.S. Vygotsky, Vol 1: Problems of General Psychology*, trans. Norris Minnik (New York: Plenum, 1987).

22. Dahlia Zaidel, "Art and Brain: Insights from Neuropsychology, Biology and Evolution," *Journal of Anatomy* 216, no. 2 (2010): 177–183.

23. Spinka, Newberry, and Bekoff, "Mammalian Play," p. 141.

24. See Mary A. Glynn, "Effects of Work Task Cues and Play Task Cues on Information Processing, Judgment, and Motivation," *Journal of Applied Psychology* 79, no 1 (1994): 34–45; Teresa M. Amabile, *Creativity in Context* (Boulder, CO: Westview Press, 1996); Charalampos Mainmelis and Sarah Ronson, "Ideas are Born in Fields of Play: Towards a Theory of Play and Creativity in Organizational Settings," *Research in Organizational Behavior* 27 (2006): 81–131; James E. Johnson, "Play and Creativity." Paper presented at the Play and Creativity Conference. Tainan, China, May 30–31, 2007.

25. Mark C. Carnes, *Minds on Fire: How Role-Immersion Games Transform College* (Cambridge, MA: Harvard University Press, 2014), p. 64.

26. Janna Jackson, "Game-based Teaching: What Educators can Learn from Videogames," *Teaching Education* 20, no. 3 (2009): 291–304.

27. Mihalyi Csikszentmihalyi, *Flow: The Psychology of Optimal Experience* (New York: Harper Collins, 1990).

28. Kurt D. Squire, "Video-Game Literacy: A Literacy of Expertise," in *Handbook of Research on New Literacies*, Ed. Michele Knobel, Colin Lankshear, Donald J. Leu, and Julie Coiro (London: Routledge, 2014), p. 653; see also John C. Beck and Mitchell Wade, *Got Game: How the Gamer Generation is Reshaping Business Forever* (Boston: Harvard Business School Press, 2004).

29. This statement is made realizing that it is completely anecdotal and unsupportable. However, it is, perhaps, still true.

30. Sidney P. Marland, *Education of the Gifted and Talented Volume 1*. Department of Health Education and Human Welfare, Office of Education, Washington DC: ERIC ED 056 243, 1971, pp. ix–x.

31. John F. Feldhusen, "Synthesis of Research on Gifted Youth," *Educational Leadership* 46, no. 6 (1989): 6–11.

32. James A. Kulik and Chen-Lin Kulik, "Synthesis of Research on Effects of Accelerated Instruction," *Educational Leadership* 42, no. 2 (1984): 84–89.

33. Feldhusen, "Synthesis of Research," p. 8.

34. Sally Reis et al., *Why Not Let High Ability Students Start School in January: The Curriculum Compacting Study*, Monograph, National Research Center on the Gifted and Talented, University of Connecticut, Mansfield: Research Monograph 93106, 1993.

35. Francis X. Archambault et al., *Regular Classroom Practices with Gifted Students: Results of a National Survey of Classroom Teachers*. Research monograph 93102. University of Connecticut, Mansfield: Storrs, 1993; Karen Westberg et al., *An Observational Study of Instructional and Curricular Practices Used with Gifted and Talented Students in Regular Classrooms*, Monograph, National Research Center on the Gifted and Talented, University of Connecticut, Mansfield: Research Monograph 93104, 1993.

36. Ed Hootstein, *Differentiation of Instructional Methodologies in Subject-Based Curricula at the Secondary Level*. Report, Metropolitan Educational Research Consortium, Richmond, VA: ERIC Document Reproduction Service No. ED 427 130, 1998.

37. Another aspect to consider here is the conversion of AP courses into college credits. This acceleration dogma might mean that an Honors student spends as little as two years actually in their program before graduating with their undergraduate degree.

38. Ethnography is the reporting mode of anthropology and integrates a record of cultural immersion in the field with comparative analysis of sociocultural patterns of behavior for the purpose of understanding the underpinnings of social interaction and cultural performance.

39. For the purposes of the simulation described below the specific named goods in this category are somewhat fictionalized as is their distribution throughout the islands.

40. Marcel Mauss, *The Gift: The Form and Reason for Exchange in Archaic Societies* (New York: Norton, 2000); Annette Weiner, *Inalienable Possessions: The Paradox of Keeping-While-Giving* (Berkley: University of California Press, 1992).

41. Hans-Georg Gademer, *Truth and Method* (New York: Continuum, 1994).

42. This is a classic "zero-sum" game in game theory. It demonstrates that two "rational" individuals may not cooperate even if it is in their best interests to do so.

43. Jackson, "Game-based Teaching," p. 296.

44. Ibid.

45. Ibid.

46. Bernice Braid, "Introduction," in *Place as Text: Approaches to Active Learning*, Ed. Bernice Braid and Ada Long, NCHC Monograph (Lincoln, NE: National Collegiate Honors Council, 2000), pp. 5–7.

47. Robert Emerson, Rachel Fretz, and Linda Shaw. *Writing Ethnographic Fieldnotes* (Chicago: University of Chicago Press, 1995).

48. Creede Lambard and Sharleen Lambard, "Caravan to Ein Arris," *Warehouse 23,* accessed October 27, 2014, http://www.sjgames.com/ill/img/retailerimages/Munchkin%20OTD/Game%20Support/GURPS/Caravan_to_Ein_Arris.pdf.

49. Roland Barthes, "Introduction to the Structural Analysis of Narratives," in *A Barthes Reader*, Ed. Susan Sontag. London: Cape, 1982; Barbara Hardy, "Towards a poetics of Fiction: 3) An Approach through Narrative." *Novel* 2, no. 1 (1968): 5–14.

50. Anthony P. Kerby, *Narrative and the Self* (Bloomington: Indiana University Press, 1991), p. 3ff.

51. NCHC, "Definition of Honors Education."

Chapter 6

Up the Hill Backward

Meeting the Challenges of Creating a Humanities Lab

Sarah Harlan-Haughey

As institutions place more and more emphasis on the importance of undergraduate research, honors programs are well positioned to help facilitate meaningful experiential learning.[1] Ready precedents and models have been set in the STEM fields, and social scientists can often see their way to creating lab structures that work for honors undergraduates. But how does one create a forum for collaborative research in the humanities? Traditional models of research in the humanities are fairly solitary affairs, involving only one or two people.

This chapter describes some the challenges and benefits of imagining and creating humanities labs in honors, where a team of motivated and gifted undergraduates collaboratively research and write about a central concern, preferably one that is relevant to the region. Honors programs and colleges often have resources, agility, and institutional support, and are thus able to experiment and innovate relatively easily.[2]

The chapter will show different models of group research in the humanities and weigh the benefits and drawbacks of each, ultimately describing and outlining the model selected for the current undergraduate lab the author created at her honors college. The chapter will also show the ways in which this innovative humanities lab has worked, and outline areas for future refinement that may suggest ways in which other researchers might build upon the model of a hybrid humanities lab.

The first section of the chapter explores the institutional pressures and expectations for fostering undergraduate research in honors, using the University of Maine's policies as a test case. Unfortunately, while the new institutional expectations for undergraduate research are fairly clear, paths to creating viable structures for such research in the humanities are not. Capstones emerging from in-class work have long been models for undergraduate work in the humanities, but this model no longer seems adequate, as it doesn't compare to a student's experience in a more formal lab, offering physical space and a time set aside solely for research.

The second section of the essay outlines models for humanities labs, weighing the benefits and drawbacks of each. The chapter will describe various models that create active-learning structures for undergraduates and that take steps toward the collaborative lab model while still, ultimately, returning to the old one-on-one mentorship structure of the humanities capstone. Special attention is paid to the following factors: level of student involvement, institutional visibility, cost, instructor responsibility, and sustainability over the course of several years with rapid turnover in the undergraduate lab's pool.[3]

The ultimate model decided upon was a humanities "lab" for undergraduate research, where a team of honors undergraduates research and write about a central concern. There are many ways to structure a humanities lab, but in this particular case, a five-person research team began active research on the body of cultural artifacts surrounding contemporary and historical hermits in Maine after the "North Pond Hermit's" decades-long retreat into the Maine woods came to light.[4]

This research team—each in charge of a chapter of the final monograph—meets regularly on a hybrid online "lab" and in person around a table in an archival library during scheduled hours every week. Beyond this regular meeting structure, each student must do her own research and fieldwork using resources and archives unique to the state of Maine. Students can also at times serve as assistants as in a science lab. But the research topic evolves and is shaped by each lab member's concerns, not by the faculty alone.

This chapter is by nature anecdotal, though it does draw extensively on others' research. This admittedly runs somewhat against the grain of this book, which aims to bring a more systematic and holistic view to bear on the question of the future of Honors. However, the personal story of a humanist asked to lead many research projects in honors serves as a way to explore issues that challenge honors colleges everywhere.

Specifically, this chapter provides the story of one medievalist at the University of Maine searching for a way to do undergraduate research that shows how colleges can help create forums for humanists to sponsor many research projects simultaneously, thus meeting many universities' mandates that visible undergraduate scholarship should take precedence over individual research or even graduate study. Arguably, the successful honors college of the future will incorporate experiential learning in the humanities that moves beyond specific disciplines while still drawing on faculty strengths and training.

The final portion of this chapter explores the successes and challenges of the humanities lab research structure. While the lab model gives students flexibility in the research they choose to do and in the timeline for completion, it does perhaps give students 'enough rope to hang themselves.' Also, while the model allows for movement and personnel change and recruitment to the lab, it makes a clear end-date for production of monographs or other products seem more and more difficult to impose.

The chapter will thus conclude with an outline of strategies others could use to offset some of these challenges, and offer a set of guidelines and suggestions that others in honors might use to create their own idiosyncratic humanities labs on their home campuses.

THE HUMANITIES UNDERGRADUATE RESEARCH QUANDARY

Administration at public universities has increasingly emphasized interdisciplinarity in hiring policies, partly as a means of making more out of less.[5] Many honors faculty are now hired as interdisciplinarians, and serve as advisors for many different kinds of undergraduate research. For example, the positions recently formed at this author's institution, place as much emphasis on "fostering undergraduate research" as they do on furthering the job candidate's own research agenda.[6]

The ad for the job this author currently holds strongly emphasized undergraduate research:

> The focus of these positions is undergraduate teaching, both in the specific discipline and in interdisciplinary Honors courses. These Preceptors will also foster research opportunities and creative activities of upper-level graduates. . . . The faculty member will develop and maintain a program of scholarship that engages undergraduate student research and Honors theses.[7]

Although this job description may seem fairly clear, it is harder than it seems for those occupying such positions to define the stated terms—and live up to their expectations. In this particular case, a series of clarifying conversations over the last four years of this author's job have determined that, although the advertising copy does not specify a specific quantity or kind of undergraduate research the candidate must foster, the institutional expectation is that at least half of the evaluated research output be connected to undergraduate work in some way.

At times it seems the focus is implicitly on quantity of advisees, honors theses, and happy and successful honors graduates, not necessarily on quality. There seems to be an inverse relationship between the amount of undergraduate research one can foster and its specificity and success. This new emphasis on faculty who must foster a significant number of honors research projects can cause issues. This is potentially a problematic requirement for instructors trained in many humanities disciplines—tenure-stream, fixed-contract, and contingent—where focused, detailed and specialized individual work has been the norm for centuries.[8]

Many humanists gain their PhDs after a protracted individual research and dissertation process, with varying levels of input and collaboration from their graduate advisor and the committee. Their work is their own and they work on it, essentially, alone—although hopefully with the close input and advice of their mentors. Many enter their first teaching jobs with such a model for research and mentorship in mind—as this author did.[9]

This does not mean this historical model is the best way to be a humanist, nor do preserves of the STEM research models inherently suggest it is the wrong way to go about things, though many recent humanist manifestos have called for the planned obsolescence of such introverted models of scholarship.

There are a few innovative programs where advanced researchers bounce ideas off one another but these remain gregarious exceptions to a solitary rule.[10] So what is a humanist to do in a brave new world where visible undergraduate research, over personal scholarship or graduate success, has become a priority, and perhaps for good reason? In the specific case of this author, the discipline of medieval literature's requisite skills of paleography, medieval language, and literary and philological criticism, are highly specialized, and difficult to teach or largely irrelevant to a noncareer audience.

For example, one can teach a class of Chaucer students to read Middle English, but one can't expect them to read Old Norse, Medieval Latin, or English older than Chaucer's in a semester. Nor should they, as undergraduates take such classes to gain a basic knowledge of medieval literature, language, and culture, not to become medievalists themselves.

The difficult question for this author, when she accepted her exciting new job as a joint hire between an Honors College and an English Department was how to create opportunities for individualized research with students. The other members of the cohort of joint hires—a journalist, social psychologist, and a political scientist—worked in fields directly applicable to "the real world" and, perhaps more significantly, to students' future careers.

Their research mentoring docket filled up more quickly than they expected while the medievalist sat on many committees, but advised few theses. This is a classic problem for humanists in honors who sincerely desire to "foster undergraduate research" as directed, but wonder how to enact the mandate of the modern university, and many honors programs, of turning out *many* happy customers.

Humanists are built to turn out a *select few* happy customers. Honors students must do innovative work, feel they have achieved something important, have preferably expanded their horizons in a significant interdisciplinary experience, and had collegial fun along the way. The old humanities mode of one-on-one mentorship seems harder and harder in the modern honors college. In this case, most students who might want to work with a medievalist are unlikely to want to make a career as a medievalist or literary scholar, so what use is specialized training to them at the thesis stage of their education?

It became increasingly apparent to this author that achieving an equitable balance between interested parties—administration/university, faculty, and undergraduate mentees—is quite difficult when following the tried-and-true humanities model. But if one could follow the lead of other researchers in similar quandaries and borrow innovative approaches from other disciplines, think creatively about one's own toolkit of skills, and work with the resources already available on campus, it might be possible to give many undergraduates an exceptional research experience.

Moreover, the innovation one might achieve could justify one's job and the allocation of valuable campus resources to the honors program, as well as create new paradigms that could be emulated on campus and elsewhere. Honors programs often have some power on campus, and nationwide are often touted as centers for innovation. As they frequently benefit from sparse resources that traditional programs desperately need, they are also ethically beholden to help find solutions for the entire institution.[11]

Ultimately, this author created an interdisciplinary humanities lab that allowed many honors undergraduates majoring in multiple fields to collaborate on interrelated research, with a goal of co-publication of a co-authored book. The following sections will detail the experimentation with multiple formats for an undergraduate humanities lab experience, followed by a brief account of the serendipity that allowed this author to find a common subject for research, a description of the humanities lab as it currently exists, and finally, an evaluation of the lab's hybrid research model.

SETTLING ON A MODE FOR LAB RESEARCH

This section will discuss the kinds of collaborative groups considered before settling on the current research structure of the hybrid lab. This author first experimented with a generative reading group, as this was the extracurricular collaborative learning space with which she was most familiar thanks to her own training as a medievalist.

Since scholars of the medieval world often need to be able to read many languages, they often find it useful to meet weekly with experts in a casual setting and to read as much as possible in a mixed skill-level group. This allows practice with pronunciation, vocabulary, and offers the expert's advice in subjects that may deserve more research—many academic papers are born in reading groups.

This author's medieval reading group has been and is popular among English majors and honors students, and it certainly does generate research relationships between the instructor and the participants. However, despite attempts to use the group as a launching pad for collaborative research projects, students tend to want to work with the professor individually on specific research questions of their own devising. Thus this model of collaborative research, though enjoyable and useful for all, has not yet solved the inherent numbers problem for humanities research.

With mixed results, the author also experimented with another mode of collaborative research, forming a team of undergraduates who worked together on a subject related to, and growing out of, a mutual class experience with the standardized honors college curriculum. A perennial challenge of a typical "Great Books" honors curriculum like the one used at UMaine is balancing the tensions between close reading, coverage, thematic relevance to current issues, and the honors courses' responsibilities as replacements for general education courses.

In an effort to lend the first two semesters of "Honors Civilizations" some much needed thematic cohesion, more clearly satisfy the replacement general education values, and explicitly link our readings with modern environmental concerns, an interdisciplinary team of thinkers—three undergraduates and this author—developed a multidisciplinary, multitechnology learning platform which emphasized environmental issues inherent in the first year's readings.

Using a class blog, the team's online environmental discussion paralleled in-class discussion and provided space for students to work out ideas before class, thus sparking substantive discussion. The team developed a series of student-created assignments, readings, images, and links that more clearly demonstrate the relevance of the past as a means of illuminating modern environmental issues.

This was a success in that it engaged promising undergraduates in research and service to the honors community and allowed them to have a positive impact on the honors curriculum, but it did not have inherent longevity or staying power. Although students seemed excited about the work, and it resulted in conference presentations and papers, it doesn't lend itself as inspiring subject matter to "spinoffs," or ultimately result in research collaborations that could become senior theses. Thus, it is certainly a visible and viable mode of collaborative research, but it is close-ended in its very nature and is not sustainable though many generations of honors cohorts.

Three other possible modes considered were a lecture series growing out of a special-interest club, group study abroad, and an online digital humanities lab.[12] The third option, the online or digital humanities lab, is a tried-and-true response to the so-called "crisis in the humanities" and one that has worked for many different kinds of programs.[13] This approach simply did not play to this author's strengths as a scholar and mentor.

Part of the process of "climbing up the hill backward" to create a collaborative research model for students, is thinking hard about one's strengths and weaknesses as a teacher and scholar. This author's strengths are in-person collaboration, Socratic dialogue, an ability to "dig in" to challenging material as a group, and enthusiasm. Among her weaknesses are digital communication and technology in general. Therefore, the straight digital humanities labs simply did not play to the strengths and training this author received. This is likely true for many other humanists at other institutions.

Moreover, students drawn to a medievalist as a teacher of "old things" do not want the romance of that experience ruined by putting in (more) long hours in front of a screen, however cool the material, without enough analog in-person interaction. This author is not a programmer, is not compelled to map things digitally, create digital editions or databases, or explore big data approaches to the humanities. This model is certainly viable for some, but not for all. Honors administrators should note digital humanities labs will not be the salvation of the humanities, as they do not encourage many valuable and relatively old-fashioned modes of engagement.[14]

The hermit humanities lab as it currently exists is a result of this experimentation—after trying out many models, this author decided on a combination of them all, using the unique and largely untouched archival material discussed in the following section. The humanities research group meets in person frequently in the Maine Folklife Archives, where it engages in reading-group style discovery of the archive's contents. The members also workshop and brainstorm as a group.

Students do fieldwork, which, although not study abroad, involves similar intercultural experience. In-person team interaction is supplemented by online blog collaboration, workshopping, and one-on-one mentoring. This gives the best balance of innovative interdisciplinarity, accessibility, specificity, research impact, and long-term sustainability.[15] The following section will describe the genesis of this lab structure.

The process of creating this unique lab is described in detail under the assumption that readers might adopt similar methods to help rethink their institutional policies and structures. Arguably, a humanities lab that focuses on local issues and resources is an innovative and cost-effective way to do this. Directors and teachers at many different levels of honors programs could make use of this model. For example, a community college honors program might be able to create an ongoing humanities lab that explores regional events and places just as easily as a private liberal arts college or a large public university.

FINDING COMMON GROUND

As it became increasingly clear that success in this new kind of job was dependent on one's creativity and ingenuity in creating new modes of research that did not require an entirely new set of research interests, this author began exploring topics that would bring a larger number of students to work in the lab and modes of research that would work best for a team of majors across many disciplines. Many required larger research libraries and special collections budgets than the state school could afford or than were geographically accessible. But then, a serendipitous local news item filled the national airwaves.

Only an hour away from the college town of Orono, Maine, a man named Chris Knight, previously referred to in local legend and scuttlebutt as the North Pond Hermit, was discovered to have been living in the Maine woods in a hidden camp for decades, stealing selectively from surrounding rustic vacation homes and camps. Everyone was fascinated by this character—he just seemed so "Maine!"

He was also reminiscent of medieval outlaws like Robin Hood and Gamelyn, characters this author had been researching for years. Perhaps here was an opportunity for a crossover project. After all, as a researcher interested in oral traditions this author had been volunteering at the Maine Folklife Center since beginning her job at the University of Maine, and had become deeply interested in the traditional culture of Maine.

The hurriedly-formed 'hermit group' quickly began active research on the folklore surrounding contemporary and historical hermits in Maine. A research team of majors from various programs was assembled—each in charge of a chapter of the final monograph. Although the research topic was local, this author's previous research on outlaw literature in the Middle Ages seemed to position her well as a director of this research question.

The lab was framed as a place for explorations of hermits as a phenomenon in Maine, asking each student to choose a research topic related to the bigger question. This research team—each in charge of a chapter of the final monograph—meets regularly online and in person. Beyond this regular meeting structure, each student must dig into the Folklife Center archives, visit regional historical centers, and interview local sources about regional legends about hermits, reporting back to the lab and sharing data with the other lab members.

Maine has long been seen as a place apart from the rest of the Northeast and New England, with its own traditions, sensibilities, and priorities. Perhaps nowhere is this more apparent than in the long Maine tradition of stories and songs about hermits. Maine hermits, in many ways Mainers look to hermits as exemplars of the purest distillation of the Maine way of life.

In their perceived ability to make do, their connection to nature, their mistrust of human change and impact, their idiosyncratic philosophies, and even in their deaths, hermits perform—or are made to perform—Maine identity in a unique and indispensable way.

The book this undergraduate team is developing will offer a survey of some of the most notable hermits in Maine history, as the lab members sort through oral histories, stories, songs, and pictures to explore the complex and ever evolving relationship between "normal" Mainers and the hermits they talk about. The group aims to discover ways in which hermits provide a forum for reification of community values—that is, distrust of disruptive innovation and rapid environmental change and the reinforcement of sense of traditional community and the possibility of dignified poverty, among other things—and Maine identity.

The book is thematically organized into chapters that focus on aspects of the Maine hermit phenomenon. Particularly salient individuals will represent each chapter's concerns, but authors illustrate our points with anecdotes from other hermit narratives, as well, thus interweaving a tapestry of Maine hermit identity. This book is not so much a history as it is a meditation on the stories told about them over time; the group is looking at firsthand accounts, papers, and the plentiful resources of the Maine Folklife Center and local historical societies.

This project makes use of archives in the university's special collections and the Folklife Center's archives, but it also requires a great deal of field work. The undergraduate team travels all over Maine to visit historical societies, local libraries and museums, and interview locals. The lab has already completed some of this research, exploring the local resources and corralling that material, as well as visiting four sites of hermit activity throughout Maine. But as with any legitimate study the group needs more data, and to spend a lot more time traveling around Maine, contacting people to interview, and exploring resources at local sites of hermit activity.

With the recent discovery of the "North Pond Hermit's" exploits, the time is right for an accessibly written survey of the unique traditions in Maine concerning hermitry. The project has already been of great interest throughout the state catalyzing interesting conversations about Maine identity, the notion of wilderness, and questions of conservation. Students' current work has been promoted and disseminated state-wide, thus showing how research in the humanities can yield results that can add nuance to Maine's history and traditions.

Nevertheless, though this humanities lab is still going and viable after two years, this author has noticed some problem areas that she is closely watching and documenting for improvement. The following section will offer an honest evaluation of the positive and negative aspects of this lab structure for the sake of others considering a similar research model.

CHALLENGES OF THE LAB MODEL

The biggest challenge to the informal hybrid lab structure is the busy lives of honors students who may be excited about the project but struggle to find extra time in their day to devote to it. As the lab is not credit-based, there is no requirement to attend. At a certain point in every semester, ambition and a sense of duty or loyalty to the lab leader lose out to graded coursework with more immediate deadlines, and the director can sit alone in the lab during scheduled weekly meetings. This is, of course, as it should be. Thus, others developing analogous labs should make the humanities lab experience part of the credit system in honors.

Another challenge to humanities labs aiming for publication is the lack of a set end-date. Students are free to define their own interests, commit the amount of time they can afford, and produce drafts and presentations as they see fit. This lab group projects completing or book in approximately four years, but that seems like a distant goal to young scholars. This sense of expansive time to complete projects—not great for overscheduled and anxious undergraduates—is ameliorated by constant opportunities for research presentations.

One can counteract this lack of real deadlines for the project with external carrots, such as presentation at conferences. If students know they have a presentation coming up, they want it to be good, and will work to finish their work enough to make it presentable—thus lab leaders should make sure each student presents her research every year at an undergraduate conference or local event. They should also work closely with each researcher to ensure that individual projects within the larger structure can come to an end when necessary.

As students navigate a world of new information and begin to do their own fieldwork and to create a workable chapter subject, they develop their own interests and research agendas, often tangential to the book project. In other words, spinoffs happen. In this unique case, though the lab director, of course, wants to see chapter drafts for our volume, she does feel compelled to encourage these spinoffs, as she believes inspired research is completed research, and that undergraduates should be protected from overspecialization—they'll encounter enough of that at graduate school, should they choose that route.

Spinoffs often end up becoming more of a one-on-one mentorship than the innovative group research model, but so far, those who have spun off are still able to report back to the group at large, as their modified research interests still relate to the lab's research content. At times, however, student interest fundamentally changes, and undergraduates move away from the research group entirely. Most of their work can be handed on to a newcomer, who is sure to make her own mark on the project. Thus humanities labs must allow one student to hand off research to another; using shared platforms like Google docs or a blog can help with transition.

Unlike more conventional labs, there is no official dedicated physical space for the group work and it has been possible to cobble together a meeting place in the archives only with the generous tolerance of the Folklife Center's director. In the future, this author would like to find a place to meet that is available for more than a few hours, thus making the lab more 'official' for the students and to better emulate the real working conditions of a laboratory.

Similarly, unlike more conventional labs, the hermit lab has no official funding or dedicated institutional support. The author supports the group members' fieldwork with her own research allowance, the occasional undergraduate research fellowship, and at times, other university-wide funds, which, although ephemeral, are often relatively easy to secure with vigilance and constant application. For example, the hermit lab is currently supported by a generous grant from the university's newly created bastion of the humanities, the University of Maine Humanities Center.[16]

Everything the lab group now has or uses was cobbled together or custom fit for the project. This, as is likely apparent, has its disadvantages, most crucially that, as in other institutions, though the university's zeitgeist is emphasizing the importance of undergraduate research and interdisciplinarity, the supportive infrastructure is simply not there yet.[17]

The cynics among us, this author included, have reason to believe many institutions may never put their money where their mouth is, so to speak. But this radical freedom allows the little research group to be beholden to no one and to have a certain agility and spontaneity it certainly would lack if it were absorbed more completely into institutional structures.[18] The following section will detail these advantages.

ADVANTAGES OF THE HUMANITIES LAB

A great advantage of this lab's focus on regional questions is its clear impact on and value to Maine's regional community. The university president's agenda for the last few years has been to emphasize the university's role as a community servant. The hermit project is valuable to the Maine community, as it serves as a means of allowing Mainers to reflect on their heritage and present values. This community and local focus has made the project appealing to administrators, prominent community members, and even donors. Members of the lab have spoken at university fundraisers, special events, and community events.

This means a happy administration and peer committee—they see the project as meeting the mandate of this author's contract, and as an attractive, topical study that doesn't need to be justified because it is an "irrelevant" humanities project; the value to Maine is clear. Even more significantly, the local focus of the lab allows students to directly see the impact and relevance of their work. The project is already visible at this early stage, as students have presented their research within the Maine community and at national conferences, and it should become even more so in the coming years as the authors move toward publication.

Other advantages are that active-learning structures for undergraduates allow them to take charge of their research, and learn from and with one another, not just their director. Labs are highly visible on the institutional level, as each member's good work validates the team's and the honors program in general.

In addition, if constructed carefully, humanities labs can cost very little, be sustainable over many years (several generations of capstone students) and allow mentors to conserve their energies. Professors with highly specialized research interests can think creatively about the application of their expertise and gain more diverse mentees. This author finds she has more time, more students, and that they produce better work, as they benefit from the collaborative experience and expertise of the entire team.[19] And, perhaps most importantly, she doesn't feel that she has lost touch with many of her specialist skills.

CONCLUSION: CLIMBING THE HILL BACKWARD

This author's experience in creating a viable humanities lab was, admittedly, all out of order. She had, so to speak, to climb up the hill backward, thinking on her feet and retrofitting a research model that could satisfy her job requirements, her own standards as a teacher and researcher, her students' needs, and perhaps most importantly, the unique character and resources of her own university. She believes that other humanists may be able to do similar work. Hopefully the educational details of her experience make other humanists' awkward but necessary climb less of a surprise.

Other lab creators could think about using this locally-sourced model while building it bigger and better, perhaps, for example, using Todd Presner's model of a humanities lab that is a "vertically integrated project team composed of graduate and undergraduate students, faculty, librarians, technologists, and review boards."[20]

Such a group could be sustainable even when a leading mentor left the lab. Other honors programs and especially other humanists affiliated with honors programs should consider the challenges and benefits of imagining and creating humanities labs, where a team of motivated and gifted undergraduates collaboratively research and write about a central concern.

Many similar labs could be created at other institutions; the honors college of the future could become a hotbed for local, vibrant, and innovative humanities research. This kind of engaged research will support the community and make stronger honors programs. Engage your honors program in a conversation about creating and supporting such innovative research groups. Brainstorm about untapped local resources like the Folklife Archives at the University of Maine, which could provide food for research projects in diverse disciplines. Your lab will probably end up looking quite different from the one at the University of Maine, but that, after all, is the point.

KEY IDEAS IN THIS CHAPTER

- Creating opportunities for undergraduate research is a core component of honors education, and increasingly higher education as a whole, and these expectations have translated into new mentoring responsibilities for university faculty, particularly in honors.
- Undergraduate research mentorship can be particularly difficult for faculty in humanities disciplines that require skills and methodologies that can take years to acquire, or research projects that have extended timelines.
- A "humanities lab" presents a unique hybrid model whereby logistical platforms from the social and natural sciences can be appropriated and utilized in the humanities, an innovation enabling faculty in honors and beyond to navigate challenging dual mentorship and research expectations of their positions.

NOTES

1. On this, see Craig T Cobane, "Moving Mountains: Honors as Leverage for Institutional Change," *Journal of the National Collegiate Honors Council* 12, no. 2 (2011): 101–104.

2. While others have explored labs and other collaborative structures for undergraduate research (Michael Lund and Leigha McReynolds, "The Class as Periodical: A Contemporary 'Humanities Lab'," *Pedagogy* 9, no. 2 (2009): 289–313; Reed Wilson, "Researching 'Undergraduate Research' in the Humanities," *Modern Language Studies* (2003), pp. 74–79; and Amy Koritz, "Futures for the Humanities," *ESC: English Studies in Canada* 33, no. 1 (2007): 239–252, among others), every situation is distinct and dictated by institutional priorities, and more importantly, local resources and interests.

3. See Jordan LaBouff's comment on undergraduates as a "flash in the pan," in Robert W. Glover, Charlie Slavin, Sarah Harlan-Haughey, Jordan P. LaBouff, Justin D. Martin, Mimi Killinger, and Mark Haggerty, "The Genesis of an Honors Faculty: Collective Reflections on a Process of Change," *Honors in Practice* 8 (2012): 157–210, 205.

4. On The North Pond Hermit, see Christopher Cousins, "'He's Surreal': Officers Amazed at 'Hermit' Burglar's Survival in Maine Woods for 27 years," *Bangor Daily News*, April 10, 2013, http://bangordailynews.com/2013/04/10/news/state/its-surreal-hes-surreal-officers-amazed-at-hermit-burglars-ability-to-survive-in-maine-woods-for-27-years/?ref=relatedSidebar; and Michael Finkel, "The Strange and Curious Tale of the Last True Hermit," *GQ*, September, 2014.

5. On the rise of interdisciplinarity as a prerequisite for hiring, see Jerry A. Jacobs, "Interdisciplinary Hype," *The Chronicle of Higher Education*, Nov 22, 2009, accessed July 15, 2015, http://chronicle.com/article/Interdisciplinary-Hype/49191/.

6. For a detailed description and analysis of the kind of job that is becoming common to honors programs, see Glover et al., especially Jordan LaBouff's discussion of "The Teacher/Scholar: Undergraduate-directed research," pp. 203–204, and the job description in the appendix, pp. 209–210.

7. Cited from Glover et al., "The Genesis of an Honors Faculty," p. 210.

8. UMaine's Honors College has admittedly been ahead of the historic curve in innovative interdisciplinarity and collaborative research between students and faculty. See, for example, Mimi Killinger's interdisciplinary collaboration, as a historian, with an art student: Mimi Killinger and Aya Mares, "Fertile Ground: Reflections on Collaborative Student-Faculty Research in the Arts," *Honors in Practice* 6 (2010): 203–206, and Charlie Slavin's manifesto on effective Honors programs as collaborative and interdisciplinary research centers: Charles Slavin, "Defining Honors Culture," *Journal of the National Collegiate Honors Council* 9, no. 1 (2008): 15–18, 16.

9. On the solitary nature of the humanities, and the need for labs and more collaboration, see Gina Hiatt, "We Need Humanities Labs," (2005) *Inside Higher Ed*, accessed July 10, 2015, https://www.insidehighered.com/views/2005/10/26/hiatt. See also Cathy N. Davidson, "What If Scholars in the Humanities Worked Together, in a Lab?" *The Chronicle of Higher Education*, May 28, 1999 45 (38), p. B4.

10. See, for example, the websites for these prestigious centers and societies for the humanities, all of which encourage regular discussion and collaboration: http://townsendcenter.berkeley.edu/programs/collaborative-research-seminars, http://www.arts.cornell.edu/sochum/about_shc.html, http://www.humcenter.pitt.edu/programs/faculty-collaborative-research-projects.php.

11. On the tricky issues of honors funding and their roles as instigators of change, see K. Celeste Campbell, "Allocation of Resources: Should Honors Programs Take Priority?" *Journal of the National Collegiate Honors Council* 6, no. 1 (2005): 95–103, and Cobane, "Moving Mountains," pp. 101–104.

12. This author developed a series of other classroom innovations that tend to spill over into long-term research interests in honors students, detailed in the article,

"Against Teleology in an Honors 'Great Books' Curriculum," *Honors in Practice* 10 (2014): 95–107.

13. A representative sample of the many current writings on the benefits and drawbacks of digital humanities labs would include David M. Berry, "The Computational turn: Thinking about the Digital Humanities," *Culture Machine* 12, no. 0 (2011); E. Leigh Bonds, "Listening in on the Conversations: An Overview of Digital Humanities Pedagogy," *CEA Critic* 76, no. 2 (2014): 147–157; Diane M. Zorich, "70 Digital Humanities Centers: Loci for Digital Scholarship," Washington, DC: Council on Library and Information Resources. (2009), accessed July 15, 2015 at http://www.clir.org/pubs/resources/promoting-digital-scholarship-ii-clir-neh/zorich.pdf; and Amy Koritz, "Futures for the Humanities," *ESC: English Studies in Canada* 33, no. 1 (2007): 239–252.

14. That is, if the humanities need saving at all. For a refreshing alternative interpretation of the "crisis in the humanities," see Christopher Panza and Richard Schur, "To Save the Humanities, Change the Narrative," *The Chronicle of Higher Education*, October 20, 2014, accessed June 12, 2015, http://chronicle.com/article/To-Save-the-Humanities-Change/149513/.

15. Others have explored and created models for humanities labs, and this author has drawn upon their knowledge and expertise in the struggle to create something that works. See especially R Wilson, "Researching 'Undergraduate Research' in the Humanities" for a survey of approaches.

16. See the Humanities Center's website for yet another example of a model for collaboration across the Humanities and beyond: http://umaine.edu/umhc/.

17. The university's strategic "Blue Sky Plan" (available at: http://umaine.edu/bluesky/) emphasizes community outreach, interdisciplinarity, and creative use of scarce resources, and this project was, in part, developed to appeal to those institutional goals. This direct appeal to topical interests has not yet resulted in institutional space or resources.

18. See Davidson and Goldberg in their article "Engaging the Humanities" where they argue against the institutionalization of interdisciplinary projects like the one outlined here. They prefer a scenario where "such interdisciplinary institutional arrangements would come and go, transact and transform in vigorous relation to the vicissitudes of the problematic objects of study and analysis for which they exist and which they serve to illuminate. We see such interdisciplinarity as flexible and transformative, self-confident and open-ended, suggestive and servicing rather than deterministic and delimiting. It is heterogeneous, not reductionistic, pluralizing, and radically nonessentializing. And it makes connections across every area of the university including the sciences, engineering, and the professional schools" (56).

19. On the value of interdisciplinary peer review and collaboration, see Julie M. Barst et al., "Peer Review Across Disciplines: Improving Student Performance in the Honors Humanities Classroom," *Honors in Practice* 7 (2011): 127–136. On the importance of student control of the research process, see Jennifer Beard et al., "Student-Guided Thesis Support Groups," *Honors in Practice* 6 (2010): 69–72; Bouke van Gorp, Marca V. C. Wolfensberger, and Nelleke de Jong, "Setting Them Free: Students as Co-Producers of Honors Education," *Journal of the National*

Collegiate Honors Council 13, no. 2 (2012): 183–195; and Kaitlin A. Briggs, "Thesis as Rhizome: A New Vision for the Honors Thesis in the Twenty-First Century," *Journal of the National Collegiate Honors Council* 10, no. 2 (2009): 103–114.

20. Todd Presner, "The Humanities—Bigger and Bolder," *Seminar: A Journal of Germanic Studies* 20, no. 2 (2014): 154–160, 158.

Index

Page references for figures are italicized.

academic engagement, 6, 9–11
Addams, Jane, 20
Arendt, Hannah, 36
Aydelotte, Frank, 58

Carnegie Foundation, 11–13
City as Text. *See* Place as Text
civic engagement. *See* community engagement
community-based research, 6, 15, 37
community college, 31, 47, 95
community engagement, 6, 11–15, 19–25, 30, 32, 40, 41, 46, 63–64, 95
community partners, 6, 14, 32, 36, 37, 39–41, 45–47, 63
curricula, vii, 3–7, 9, 15, 29, 45, 59, 62, 93

Dewey, John, 10, 13, 29, 30, 43

equity, 32

"Four-C" model of creativity, 70, 83

Geertz, Clifford, 16
general education requirements, 54, 74
Generic Universal Role Play System (GURPS), 80–83

gifted-and-talented education, 75–77

Harkavy, Ira, 11–13
honors research, 92
Humanities Lab, 7, 89–91, 93–95, 98–100

interdisciplinarity, 30, 56, 58, 60, 63–65, 95, 99
internships, 13, 14, 44

kata, 72
Knight, Chris. *See* North Pond Hermit
Kula ring symbolic exchange system, 78, 79

lateral prefrontal cortex (LPFC), 69, 70
liberal arts, vii, 3, 30, 31, 46, 47, 56, 58, 59, 95

Meisho-Deshi, 82
mentoring, 61, 92, 95
millennials, 30
minority, 12, 61
Morrill Acts, 10

National Collegiate Honors Council (NCHC), 2, 3, 5, 14, 15, 17, 71, 73, 80
North Pond Hermit, 90, 96, 97

origin, of honors education. *See* Aydelotte, Frank

Place as Text, 4, 17, 80
Praxis Labs, 29, 31, 32, *33, 34, 35,* 36–41, 43–48
privilege, 6
Progressive Era, 10

Reacting to the Past, 71, 74, 75, 81
retention, 4, 20
rigor, 5, 62

Scholastic Aptitude Test (SAT), 76
seminars, 9, 54, 60, 61
service-research, 15
student recruitment, 4, 20, 91

undergraduate student research, 91

Wikipedia, 1, 2, 4

Zone of Proximal Development (ZPD), 73–75, 77, 80

About the Editors and Authors

EDITORS

Robert W. Glover is an assistant professor of honors and political science at the University of Maine. He studies community engagement, democratic participation, and immigration policy and has published in a wide range of disciplinary journals and edited volumes. He is also an active researcher and innovator in the scholarship of teaching and learning having co-edited in 2012 (with Daniel Tagliarina) the volume, *Teaching Politics Beyond the Book: Films, Texts, and New Media in the Classroom*. He is a 2014 recipient of the Douglas Harward Faculty Award for Service-Learning Excellence given by the organization Maine Campus Compact and was recognized by the Maine State Senate for his innovative work fostering undergraduate community-based policy research.

Katherine M. O'Flaherty is an honors faculty fellow at Barrett, The Honors College at Arizona State University. She holds a Ph.D. in history and C.A.S. in higher education leadership from the University of Maine. O'Flaherty primarily researches immigration and refugee history from World War II to the present and has designed several upper-level honors courses that provide students the opportunity to undertake research on immigration-related issues. She also researches and teaches about issues in higher education and the ways technology intersects with teaching and learning in the humanities and the liberal arts. She was selected as a Digital Humanities Award winner for one of her curated projects in 2013.

AUTHORS

François Amar is dean of the Honors College and professor of chemistry at the University of Maine. He holds a Ph.D. in theoretical chemistry from the University of Chicago and his main research interests have been in the development and applications of computational methods to problems in phase transitions and reaction dynamics of small clusters, biofuel catalysis, and, more recently, metal mediated reactions in proteins. He has also researched active-learning strategies in STEM classrooms including the laboratory setting. Recent work in STEM education includes an exploration of the role of gesture in students' thinking and communicating about chemistry. In his role as Honors College Dean, he is interested in advancing Honors' strong liberal arts core, in fostering undergraduate research clusters in Honors, and in promoting community-engaged research. In Fall of 2013, the organizers of the Belfast (Maine) Poetry Festival paired him with artist Kris Engman to create and present their poetic and visual piece, *Water Cycle*, which explores aspects of our fascination with water. In March 2015, he co-organized the event *Poetry Speaks to Science* as part of the inaugural Maine Science Festival.

Martha Bradley-Evans is the senior associate vice president of academic affairs and dean of undergraduate studies at the University of Utah. From 2002 through 2011, she served as the dean of the University Honors College at Utah. She is also a full professor in the College of Architecture and Planning and has taught at the University of Utah since 1993. Bradley-Evans has published ten books including *Salt Lake City: Yesterday and Today* (2010) and *Plural Wife* (2012). The latter was the winner of the Utah State Historical Society's Best Documentary Book Award for 2012.

Gregory Clancey is the founding master of Tembusu College at the National University of Singapore (NUS). He also holds joint appointments as an associate professor in NUS' Dept. of History and Asia Research Institute (ARI). His Ph.D. is in the social and historical study of science and technology (from Massachusetts Institute of Technology) and his research centers on the cultural history of science and technology, particularly in modern Japan and East Asia. His book *Earthquake Nation: The Cultural Politics of Japanese Seismicity* (2006) won the Sidney Edelstein Prize from the Society for the History of Technology in 2007. He is co-editor of the textbook *Major Problems in the History of American Technology* (1998) and *Historical Perspectives on East Asian Science, Technology and Medicine* (2002).

Catelijne Coopmans is a fellow and director of studies at Tembusu College at the National University of Singapore (NUS). She is also a research fellow at the Asia Research Institute at the same university. Trained in science and technology studies (STS), she joined Tembusu when it opened its doors in 2011 and has since worked with colleagues and students to develop an engaging general education program. Her seminar classes 'Fakes' and 'Biomedicine and Society' are centrally focused on questions of evidence and valuing. Outside the classroom, she is a driving force behind Tembusu's personal development-oriented programs, and also champions discourse and initiative relating to gender/sexuality and wildlife conservation. Catelijne holds a Master's in social history of medicine and a D.Phil. in management studies from the University of Oxford. Her research, which focuses on visual evidence and on the dynamics of "revelation," has been published in STS journals and volumes.

Sarah Harlan-Haughey is assistant professor of honors and english at the University of Maine. She holds a Masters degree and Ph.D. in medieval studies from Cornell University and has diverse research and teaching interests ranging from Old English and medieval Scandinavian Literature to the interdisciplinary humanities. A graduate of an innovative honors program at the University of Montana, she is dedicated to rethinking pathways to the humanities for honors students, and especially to finding ways for students to experience art, literature, and history in a holistic way. She has published in *Honors in Practice,* and has a book forthcoming on medieval outlaw narratives as nature writing entitled *The Ecology of the Outlaw*. She publishes articles and chapters in Medieval Studies publications.

Cecile Houry is an assistant dean for external affairs in the Robert Stempel College of Public Health & Social Work at Florida International University (FIU). Prior to this, she served as the assistant vice president for FIU's Office of Engagement and director of student programs for the FIU Honors College. Houry is also a fellow faculty in the Honors College and teaches a community service-research course. She has presented on community engagement at conferences hosted by the National Collegiate Honors Council, Coalition of Urban and Metropolitan Universities, and Florida Campus Compact. She holds a Ph.D. in history from the University of Miami, Coral Gables, where her research focused on the intersection of gender and sports in the United States.

Abby Loebenberg was trained as an architect at the University of Cape Town, South Africa, earning a BA.S. and B.Arch. degree with distinction. Following this, she received a Rhodes Scholarship to Oxford University in the United Kingdom where she gained a Master's degree (M.Phil.) in material anthropology and museum ethnography and a doctorate (D.Phil.) in social and cultural anthropology. Since graduating from her doctoral program in 2011 she has taught at the University of Mississippi in the Sally McDonnell Barksdale Honors College as a Barksdale Fellow and is currently an honors faculty fellow at Arizona State University. She has published peer-reviewed articles on virtual space and play, childhood collection, playground trading and economies and on recovery of place after Hurricane Katrina. Her current research interests include the study of friendship and the use of simulations and games as part of pedagogy in higher education.

James McKusick is founding dean of the Honors College and professor of English at the University of Missouri–Kansas City (UMKC). He completed his B.A. in English and comparative literature at Dartmouth College, and his M.A., M.Phil., and Ph.D. in English at Yale University. He was previously a faculty member in the English Department at the University of Maryland, Baltimore County (1984–2005), where he also served as director of the Honors College (2002–2005). More recently, he served as dean of the Davidson Honors College at the University of Montana (2005–2015). McKusick has served as a reviewer and consultant for honors programs in Idaho, Massachusetts, Montana, Texas, and Wyoming. His research and teaching interests include British Romanticism, literary theory, environmental studies, and the history of science. He is the author of *Coleridge's Philosophy of Language* (1986) and *Green Writing: Romanticism and Ecology* (2000). He is co-editor of *Literature and Nature: Four Centuries of Nature Writing* (2001) and *Faustus: From the German of Goethe, translated by Samuel Taylor Coleridge* (2007).

Sylvia Torti is the dean of the Honors College and an associate professor (Lecturer). Torti holds a Ph.D. in biology from the University of Utah and a bachelor of arts from Earlham College. She conducted her graduate work on tropical monodominant forests in the Democratic Republic of Congo, Panama, Mexico, and Trinidad resulting in scientific publications as well as subject matter for her first novel. She wrote "The Scorpion's Tail," which won the Miguel Mármol Award for "best debut fiction by an American of Latino/a descent." She is co-director of the interdisciplinary working collective "Mapping Meaning" (www.mappingmeaning.org).

www.ingramcontent.com/pod-product-compliance
Lightning Source LLC
Chambersburg PA
CBHW021800230426
43669CB00006B/149